Think, Act,
Invest Like
Warren Buffett

THE WINNING STRATEGY TO HELP
YOU ACHIEVE YOUR FINANCIAL AND
LIFE GOALS

Larry E. Swedroe

Illustrations by Carl Richards

With Igors Alferovs and
Richard Wood

*This book is dedicated to four of the
most important people in my life,
my grandchildren—Jonathan, Sophie and
Gracie Rosen, and Ruby Jane Morris.*

Think, Act and Invest Like Warren Buffett: The Winning
Strategy to Help You Achieve Your Financial and Life Goals
Larry E. Swedroe, with Igors Alferovs and Richard Wood

ISBN: 9780077167899
e-ISBN: 9780077167905

Published by McGraw-Hill Professional
Shoppenhangers Road
Maidenhead
Berkshire
SL6 2QL
Telephone: 44 (0) 1628 502 500
Fax: 44 (0) 1628 770 224
website: www.mcgraw-hill.co.uk

British Library Cataloguing in Publication Data
A catalogue record for this book is available from the
British Library

Library of Congress Cataloguing in Publication Data
The Library of Congress data for this book is available from
the Library of Congress

Typeset by SRNova Private Limited, India
Cover design by Two Associates
Illustrations by Carl Richards

McGraw-Hill books are available at special quantity discounts.
Please contact the Corporate Sales Executive

Foreword:
A Change of Thinking
for the UK

The benefits to individuals of an evidence-based, passive approach to investing are incontrovertible; even though today, with widespread concern about excessive fees and investment costs, passive funds still only make up a modest portion of the total UK market.

At the end of 2014, passively-managed assets accounted for just 11.2 per cent of the total £834 billion assets under management. However, the £93.2 billion this percentage represents is a record for the UK and an increase of 23.5 per cent on the previous year.[1]

This increase in market share is no doubt due in part to growing demands from investors, together with some media commentators, for greater clarity regarding the cost of investing. The implementation in January 2013 of the Retail Distribution Review, which outlawed commission-based investment advice from financial advisers and made the cost of investing much more transparent to individual investors, was a significant step along the way.

However, a great deal of education and promotion is still required if British individuals are to emulate the success of their counterparts in the US, where around a third of the market is in passive funds: by the end of 2014, $4.12 trillion (29.7 per cent) was invested passively in the US, compared with $9.7 trillion invested in actively managed funds.[2]

In 2012, we established sensibleinvesting.tv to bring the message about passive investing to a UK audience and secured exclusive interviews with gurus of the industry such as John Bogle, Bill Bernstein, Ken French and Charles Ellis, along with Nobel Prize-winners Eugene Fama and William Sharpe. We were delighted when Larry Swedroe, well known in investing circles for his insightful comment and opinions on CBSnews.com's Moneywatch and IndexUniverse.com, and in his many books on the subject of investing, contacted us to comment favourably on the site. We were excited when he then invited us to work with him on adapting *Think, Act and Invest Like Warren Buffett* for a British audience.

The 'light bulb' moment, when an individual clearly sees how adopting the passive route will save him or her money, earn greater returns and provide peace of mind, has proven a real turning point for many investors. To bring this moment of clarity to more people, we firmly believe there is a real need for more authoritative, well-argued and, above all *readable* books: those which clearly explain the differences between active and passive investing and simply demonstrate how the low-cost, evidence-based approach can effectively capture market returns. As the saying goes, it is not rocket science.

This book, we suggest, hits the mark in all respects. It is aimed at anyone who is building their wealth and wants to maintain it; is confused by the 'science of investing'; and is unsure how to differentiate between worthwhile and self-serving advice. It provides the reader with a basic understanding of investment management; allows them to understand and apply the principles used by some of the world's most successful investment professionals;

and protects against the worst excesses of a self-interested industry.

We sincerely hope you enjoy, and benefit from, reading it.

IGORS ALFEROVS AND RICHARD WOOD

A Few Words About
Warren Buffett

Warren Buffett – often called the "Oracle of Omaha" – is probably the best known investor in the world today. With a net worth of around 71.7 billion dollars[1] (about £48,360,000,000) he is certainly one of the most successful.

Born in 1930 in Omaha, Nebraska, he began investing at the age of 11 and, while still a teenager, invested in his father's business and bought a farm. Today, he is the chairman, CEO and major shareholder in Berkshire Hathaway, a multinational conglomerate owning many of the world's most famous brands. His annual letter to shareholders, combining business with humour, is a much-anticipated event and is covered extensively by the financial and news media in the US and worldwide. He is also a noted philanthropist, giving more than $30 billion of his fortune to the Bill and Melinda Gates Foundation.[2]

Despite being perhaps the world's most successful active investor, Buffett is an advocate of passive investing for the individual investor who doesn't want to spend 24 hours a day watching the movement of the FTSE or Dow Jones indexes. He recognises that patience is one of the prosperous investor's biggest virtues, and that "success in investing doesn't correlate with IQ".[3]

When investing for his nearest and dearest, his instructions are very clear. The advice given in his will to the trustees of the cash he will leave to his wife stipulates, "[it] could not be more simple: put 10% of the cash in short-term government bonds and 90% in a very low cost S&P 500 index fund. I believe the trust's long term results from this policy will be superior to those attained by most investors – whether pension funds, institutions or individuals who employ high-fee managers".[4]

While most financial commentators recognise Buffett's star quality, they also recognise that he is a one-off and that "ordinary mortals" have little chance of replicating his achievements in stock-picking.[5]

Contents

Introduction:
Why I Wrote This Book

Each of my books is about what I call the "science of investing"—the evidence demonstrating the prudent investment strategy. My *Only Guides You'll Ever Need* series deals with shares, bonds, alternative investments and designing the right financial plan. My *Wise Investing* series is a collection of stories and analogies designed to demonstrate that the winning investment strategy is a simple, elegant, and logical one. And because it is so simple, requiring little effort (though lots of discipline), it is also the winning strategy in life.

What I have learned from my experiences is that not many people will devote a lot of time to learn about investing despite its importance. It is difficult to get them to read a 300-page book that cites dozens of studies. That is why I have written this book.

Think, Act and Invest Like Warren Buffett is designed to explain how adopting some basic principles can help you outperform the vast majority of investors and increase the chances of achieving your financial and life goals.

Over the years, I have talked to thousands of people about investing. I have learned there are some individuals who can be successful investors on their own. If you believe you fall into that category, Chapter 8 provides five important questions for you to answer before you decide to go it alone.

Many others have found great benefit in working with a financial planner. For those who want to consider working with an adviser, Chapter 8 also provides information on how to perform thorough due diligence as you search for a financial planner offering a fiduciary standard of care, who can truly add value, such as making sure your investment plan is part of an overall financial plan addressing estate, tax and insurance issues.

Think, Act and
Invest Like
Warren Buffett

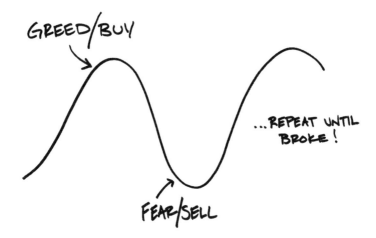

1

Want to Invest More Like Buffett? Start Taking His Advice

If investors were asked, "Who do you think is the greatest investor of our generation?" an overwhelming majority would answer, "Warren Buffett." If they were then asked, "Should you follow the advice of the person you consider the greatest investor?" you would think that they would say, "Yes!" The sad truth is that while Buffett is widely admired, the majority of investors not only fail to consider his advice, but tend to do *exactly the opposite* of what he recommends.

To demonstrate the truth of this statement, we will review Buffett's investment guidance and see if people actually have followed it. We will review his advice on three issues:

1. Whether you should invest in actively managed or passively managed mutual funds (such as index funds).

2. Whether you should listen to market forecasts.

3. Whether you should try to time the market.

Actively managed funds attempt to uncover and exploit securities the market has "mispriced", buying those they believe are undervalued and avoiding those they believe are overvalued. Actively managed funds may also attempt to time investment decisions to be more heavily invested when the market is rising and less so when the market is falling. In contrast, passively managed funds are basically buy-and-hold vehicles that avoid stock picking and market timing, believing the costs outweigh the benefits. Active investors also look to "experts" for an investing edge, while passive investors ignore such advice.

Before reviewing Buffett's advice, it is important to note that he knows that you cannot invest exactly like he does. You cannot buy entire companies and incorporate them into Berkshire Hathaway, nor can you negotiate special deals during crises, when companies such as Goldman Sachs are willing to pay "top dollar" to have Warren Buffett invest. However, you can follow his guidance about the right investment strategy. As you read Buffett's advice, ask yourself if you have been practising what he preaches.

Let's begin with Buffett's advice on which type of funds you should invest in.

ACTIVE VERSUS PASSIVE INVESTING

The following are some of the Oracle of Omaha's words of advice on this important decision:

- "By periodically investing in an index fund the know-nothing investor can actually outperform most investment professionals."[1]

- "Most investors, both institutional and individual, will find that the best way to own common stocks is through an index fund that charges minimal fees. Those following this path are *sure to beat* [emphasis mine] the net results (after fees and expenses) delivered by the great majority of investment professionals. Seriously, costs matter."[2]

- "Over the 35 years, American business has delivered terrific results. It should therefore have been easy for investors to earn juicy returns: all they had to do was piggyback Corporate America in a diversified, low-expense way. An index fund that they never touched would have done the job. Instead many investors have had experiences ranging from mediocre to disastrous."[3]

- "So many investors, brokers and money managers hate to admit it, but the best place for the average retail investor to put his or her money is in index funds."[4]

What is difficult for many investors to understand is that indexing works because *not making* investment decisions (trying to pick shares or mutual funds or trying to time the market) produces better results than making them. Of course, no one in the City would admit that. Remember, the City benefits from the higher fees and greater commissions generated by active strategies. It needs you to play the game of active management because that is its winning strategy.

THE VALUE OF FORECASTS

The following is Buffett's advice on whether you should be paying attention to the latest forecasts from so-called economic and market experts.

- "We have long felt that the only value of stock forecasters is to make fortune-tellers look good. Even now, Charlie [Munger; vice-chairman of Berkshire Hathaway] and I continue to believe that short-term market forecasts are poison and should be kept locked up in a safe place, away from children and also from grown-ups who behave in the market like children."[5]

- "A prediction about the direction of the stock market tells you nothing about where stocks are headed, but a whole lot about the person doing the predicting."[6]

- "Forming macro opinions or listening to the macro or market predictions of others is a waste of time. Indeed, it is dangerous because it may blur your vision of the facts that are truly important"[7]

Most investors find it hard to believe that their life would be better *without* so much information and that ignoring the investment noise would improve their performance. They develop a need to "tune in", listening to the BBC news, reading the *FT* or buying *Investors Chronicle*. While investors believe they are tuning in to valuable information, what they are generally hearing is nothing more than what American personal finance author Jane Bryant Quinn calls "investment porn", and what she feels were "shameless stories about performance that tickle our prurient financial interest".[8] Instead of tuning in, you should be tuning out.

Buffett implores investors to ignore forecasts because they tell you nothing about where the market is headed. Research also proves this. The following is a brief summary of that research.

- Economists' forecasting skill has been about as good as guessing. Even those who directly or indirectly run the economy — such as the Bank of England, the Treasury and, globally, the US Federal Reserve and the European Central

Bank — have forecasting records worse than pure chance. Even worse, just when you need the forecasts to be most accurate, they have been the most wrong. Economists have not predicted the turning points.[9]

- There have been no economic forecasters who consistently lead the pack in forecasting accuracy.[10]

- Increased sophistication in forecasting has not improved the accuracy of forecasts.[11]

- The only thing that relates to forecasting accuracy has been fame, and the relationship has been negative. The more famous the forecaster, the more inaccurate the forecasts.[12]

Why do investors pay attention to forecasts, ignoring the evidence and Buffett's sage advice? My experience has convinced me that this irrational behaviour is caused by an all-too-human need to believe that there is someone who can protect us from bad things, such as bear markets. Unfortunately, there is only one "person" who knows where the market is going. If we ask Him, we won't get an answer, at least not in this lifetime. And in the next one, it won't matter. This is why whenever I am asked about my forecast for the economy or the market, my answer is always the same: "My crystal ball is always cloudy."

What we have learned is that we are no closer to being able to predict the market despite all the innovations in information technology and decades of academic research. The next time you are tempted to act on some guru's latest forecast, ask yourself the following questions:

- Is Warren Buffett acting on this expert's opinion?

- If he isn't, should I be doing so?

- What do I know about the value of this forecast that Buffett (and the market in general) doesn't?

Author Carl Richards, in his book *The Behavior Gap*, recommends asking three questions before you act on someone's advice or forecast:[13]

- If I make this change and I am right, what impact will it have on my life?

- What impact will it have if I am wrong?

- Have I been wrong before?

Asking and honestly answering those questions should have you acting more like Warren Buffett and less like the majority of investors who are engaging in behaviour destructive to their portfolios.

We now turn to Buffett's advice on market timing.

MARKET TIMING

The following are some of Buffett's admonitions to those who are tempted to time the market.

- "Our favourite holding period is forever."[14]

- "Our stay-put behaviour reflects our view that the stock market serves as a relocation centre at which money is moved from the active to the patient."[15]

- "Success in investing doesn't correlate with IQ. Once you have ordinary intelligence, what you need is the temperament to control the urges that get other people in trouble investing."[16]

- "Inactivity strikes us as intelligent behaviour."[17]

It can be hard to hear that the best course of action during tough market times is to stay the course. Keeping your head while everyone else around you is losing theirs is difficult. It can be even harder to hear that message repeated while things go from bad to worse. However, the message to stay the course is worth repeating because it is the best advice. Because there is no evidence that there are good forecasters, efforts to time the market are highly unlikely to prove productive.

The great irony is that while investors idolise Buffett, they just do not listen to his advice. While investors were pulling hundreds of billions out of the stock market in the wake of the financial crisis of 2008, Buffett was buying. And while investors were once again reacting to the European crisis of 2011, withdrawing almost $100 billion from equity funds in the US alone during the six months ending October 2011, Berkshire Hathaway was investing almost $24 billion in stocks. That represented Buffett's largest commitment of new cash in at least 15 years.[18]

Buffett knows that a down market is when investors should be buying, not selling. While he admonishes investors against market timing, he does advise that if you are going to try to time the market you should buy when everyone else is fearful, and sell when everyone else is greedy. What Buffett advises is not to sell (as most individuals do) when expected returns are the greatest (because valuations are low). That is when Buffett is generally a buyer. He is not a buyer because he believes he has a clear crystal ball. Instead, he is buying because expected returns are high. "Whether we're talking about socks or stocks, I like buying quality merchandise when it is marked down."[19] Conversely, the time to be a seller is not when valuations are low and expected returns are high. Buffett offers this advice on the subject:

> "The most common cause of low prices is pessimism — sometimes pervasive, sometimes specific to a company or industry. We want to do business in such an environment, not because we like pessimism but because we like the prices it produces. It is optimism that is the enemy of the rational buyer."[20]

The time to be a seller is when the "coast is clear" and risks appear to be low. That is when valuations are high and expected returns are low. Buying low and selling high is a much better strategy than the reverse, which is what most investors do.

The appealing thing is that there is a simple strategy that allows you to act like Warren Buffett, buying when valuations are low and expected returns are high, and selling when valuations are high and expected returns are low. All you need is the discipline to ignore your emotions and adhere to your investment plan, which should require regular rebalancing. Rebalancing, or the process of restoring a portfolio to its original composition, is integral to the winning investment strategy. It requires you to buy what has done relatively poorly (at relatively low valuations) and sell what has done relatively well (at relatively high valuations). However, it is not easy to maintain the discipline to stay the course because constant "tuning in", and the emotions it causes, often get in the way.

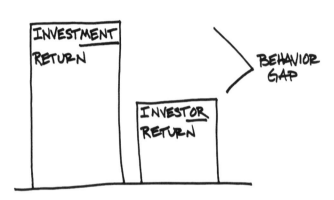

2

Want to Invest More Like Warren Buffett? Start Thinking Like He Does

In order for you to learn to invest like Warren Buffett, you have to learn how to think like him. That is what this chapter is all about. It provides you with three important insights that will help you become Buffett-like in your approach to investing. First, you'll learn the right way to think about bad news. Next, you'll learn how to avoid the mistake most investors make of engaging in what is referred to as "stage-one" thinking. Instead, you will learn to think ahead, engaging in "stage-two" thinking. And finally, you'll learn not only how important it is to have a well-developed plan but also how critical it is to adhere to it.

UNDERSTAND HOW TO THINK ABOUT BAD NEWS

One of the secrets to Buffett's success as an investor is that during bear markets he is able to keep his head while everyone else around him is losing theirs. He understands that bad news doesn't mean share prices have to go lower. The market price already reflects all publicly available information. That means that markets can be expected to continue to fall only if future news is worse than already expected. If the news is no worse than expected, you will earn high returns resulting from the low valuations. And even if the future news is not good, but is better than expected, valuations will rise as the risk premium demanded by the market begins to fall. That's often how bull markets begin.

It is totally irrelevant to share prices whether news is good or bad. Failing to understand this basic tenet causes investors to react to the news and get overenthusiastic when news is good, and panic when news is bad. In order to be a successful investor, what you need to understand is whether the news is better or worse than *already expected.* In other words, what matters is not whether news is good or bad but whether or not it is a surprise. Let's take a look at an example.

On Friday February 22, 2013, the credit rating agency, Moody's, downgraded UK government debt from AAA to AA, reflecting weakness in the UK economy and thus the ability of the government to repay its debts. The broadsheet newspapers over that weekend were full of gloomy predictions both for a spike in UK government debt yields – i.e. the rate of interest they have to pay to borrow money – and a rout of sterling in the foreign exchange markets on Monday when the markets opened again. The *Sunday Times* had the headline 'Pound in peril without AAA'. At the end of March 2013, bond yields stood at 1.8 per cent – they had actually fallen – and the pound was worth $1.52 – virtually unchanged from the day of the downgrade. The point is that the market had already made its own judgement on the state of the economy and priced in the news long before the loss of its Moody's AAA rating.

The bottom line is this: If you want to invest more like Buffett, you must understand that surprises are a major determinant of stock performance. Because they are unpredictable and instantly incorporated into prices, you are best served by ignoring the news because acting on it is likely to prove counterproductive.

AVOID STAGE ONE THINKING

One of the keys to Buffett's success as an investor is that he avoids the tendency to engage in what the American economist Thomas Sowell called "stage-one" thinking, a weakness of most investors. They see the crisis and the risks, but cannot see beyond that. Their gut instincts take over, they cannot control their emotions, panic sets in, and well-developed plans are abandoned.

On the other hand, Buffett engages in "stage-two" thinking. He expects that a crisis will lead governments and central bankers to come up with solutions to address the problem. And the greater the crisis, the greater the response is likely to be. That allows him to see beyond the crisis, enabling his head to keep control over his gut instincts and his emotions. The next time you find yourself reacting to a crisis, ask yourself the following questions:

- Am I engaging in stage-one thinking?

- Do I know something the market doesn't?

- Is the news already incorporated into prices?

- Do I want to sell when valuations are low and expected returns are high?

- Will governments and central banks do nothing or address the problem?

- Have I reacted in the past to such events? How did that turn out?

Most important, you need to ask this question: If I sell now, how will I know when it is safe to buy again? This is the big problem for those who sell during crises.

Is There Ever A "Safe" Flag?

There is another problem for those who are tempted by the latest crisis to sell and wait for less risky times. If you go to the beach to ride the waves and you want to know if it is safe, you simply look to the lifeguard station. If there's a black-and-white flag, it is safe to surf. If it is red, it is too dangerous to take a chance. For many investors, the market often looks too dangerous. So they do not want to buy, or they decide to sell.

Here is the problem. While the surfer can wait a day or two for the sea to calm down, there is never a flag saying it is safe to invest. The markets faced a litany of problems between March 2009 and March 2011. There was never a black-and-white flag. It was red the entire time. That is why investors were pulling out hundreds of billions of pounds from the market, and missed one of the greatest rallies of the last century, with the FTSE All-Share Index providing a return of more than 70 per cent. So if you decide to sell, you are virtually doomed to fail as you wait for the next "safe" flag.

Even worse is what happened to some investors who thought they saw such a flag. Consider this sad tale of an investor who watched the FTSE All-Share Index fall from about 3,748 in June 2007 all the way to 1,890 on November 21, 2008. Worn out by the wave of bad news, he sold. However, he knew there was a problem. With interest rates at their then current levels, he could not achieve his financial goals without taking risks. So he designed a strategy to get back in. He would wait until next year to see if the market recovered. By January 2, 2009, the FTSE All-Share Index had risen over 20 per cent to 2,275. Of course, he had missed that rally while he waited for that "safe" flag. But now he felt that it was once again OK to buy. Unfortunately, by March 6, 2009, the FTSE All-Share Index had dropped back all the way to 1,789. So he sold again, and the market began its fierce rally. In my opinion, he'll have a very difficult time reaching his investment goals. The problem is that once you sell you are virtually doomed to fail. The "safe" flag you are waiting for will never appear. Never. Buying when the market has gone up and selling when it has gone down explains why so many investors have taken all the risks of equities but have earned bond-like returns.

Understanding the fallibility of individual investors is why Buffett offered these words of wisdom:

- "The most important quality for an investor is temperament, not intellect."[1]

- "Investing is simple, but not easy."[2]

While it is simple to invest more like Buffett — you just need a well-designed plan and have the discipline to stick to it — it is not easy. Emotions, such as fear and panic in bear markets, and greed and envy in bull markets, cause even well-developed plans to end up in the rubbish bin. The guts take over from the head — and guts do not make good decisions.

If you want to invest more like Buffett, you are going to have to learn to control your emotions. The best way of preventing your gut instincts from taking over is to stop paying attention to forecasters and so-called experts.

HAVE A PLAN AND STICK TO IT

Warren Buffett's other passion is bridge. He once said: "I wouldn't mind going to jail if I had three cellmates who played bridge." Noting the similarity between bridge and investing, he stated: "The approach and strategies are very similar." He added: "In the stock market you do not base your decisions on what the market is doing, but on what you think is rational."[3] With bridge, you need to adhere to a disciplined bidding system. While there is no one best system, there is one that works best for you. Once you choose a system, you need to stick with it.

Similarly, with investing, in order to be successful you must have a "system", a plan that determines your asset allocation that is based on your unique ability, willingness and need to take risk. Just as there is no one best bidding system, there is no one best asset allocation. However, there is one that is right for you. Once you develop your plan, and put it in writing, you need to stick to it. Here is Buffett's advice on the subject:

> "Once you have ordinary intelligence, what you need is the temperament to control the urges that get other people into trouble in investing."[4]

INVESTORS WORSHIP BUT IGNORE THE ORACLE OF OMAHA

Having completed our review of Buffett's advice, it is time now to answer the following questions:

1. Do you act on market forecasts?

2. Do you try to time the market?

3. Have you sold after markets have experienced big losses, only to then buy again after they have recovered?

4. Have you adhered to an investment policy statement and your asset allocation, only rebalancing and tax managing as required?

If, in answering the questions above, you recognise that you have been engaging in destructive behaviour, then you have taken the first step on the road to recovery. However, because crises are the norm, you will continue to be tested. Just as there are no ex-alcoholics, just recovering ones, there are no ex-market timers, just recovering ones. That explains why while there are tens of millions of investors who idolise the Oracle of Omaha, there are few individual investors who actually act in the market like Warren Buffett. However, you can be one of the few if you make up your mind to do it.

Buffett knows that the winning investment strategy is really simple. However, he also acknowledges that it is not easy, because emotions get in the way of being able to maintain discipline and adhere to a well-developed plan.

The rest of this book is designed to help you play the winner's game, providing the simple pre-scriptions for success. The rest is up to you.

WEIGHT OF EVIDENCE

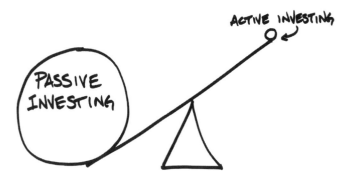

3

Should You Be an Active or a Passive Investor?

There are two competing theories about investing. The conventional wisdom is that markets are inefficient; they persistently misprice assets. If that is true, smart, hard-working people can uncover which shares the market has under or overvalued and make money by loading up on the undervalued ones or avoiding (or even shorting) overvalued ones. They can think, "BP is trading at 20 and we should load up on it because it is really worth 30" or "We should avoid it because it is really worth 10". This is called the art of share selection. And if markets misprice assets, smart people can also time the market, raising their equity allocations and getting in ahead of the bull emerging into the arena, and lowering their equity allocations before the bear emerges from its hibernation. This is called the art of market timing. Together, they make up the art of active management.

The competing theory is that *markets are efficient*. Hence, the price of a security is the best estimate of the correct price. If markets are efficient, attempts to outperform them are highly unlikely to prove productive, especially after expenses. *This does not mean it is impossible to beat the market. Given the tens of thousands of professionals (and millions of individuals) engaging in the effort, we should expect some to randomly succeed even over long periods of time.*

In order to have the best chance of achieving your financial goals, you need to decide which theory and strategy is the wisest. The problem is how to know whether an active or a passive strategy is the wisest. Despite the fact that money may be the third most important thing in our lives (not money itself, but what money provides) after our family and our health, our education system has totally failed to equip investors with the knowledge to determine the answer to our question. Unless you have an MBA in finance, it is likely that you have never taken even a single course in capital markets theory.

Additionally, you are likely to get a biased answer from either the City or the financial media. The City wants and needs you to play the game of active investing so they make money by charging high fees for active management and through commissions and bid-offer spreads whenever you trade. The financial media also wants and needs you to "tune in".

THE EVIDENCE

Fortunately, there is a large body of evidence on the inability of active management to deliver *alpha*: performance above appropriate risk-adjusted benchmarks (such as comparing the performance of a small-cap fund to a small-cap index, not to a broad equity index like the FTSE All-Share Index). As the Carl Richards sketch shows, the weight of evidence is firmly in favour of passive investing. The following are short summaries of the volumes of academic research on the efforts of individual investors, mutual funds and pension plans to generate alpha. Remember, if markets are inefficient, we should see evidence of the persistent ability to outperform appropriate risk-adjusted benchmarks. And that persistence should be greater than randomly expected.

Individual Investors

We begin with exploring the evidence on the performance of individual investors. It clearly demonstrates that individuals are playing a loser's game, enriching only the purveyors of products and services. The following is a summary of the evidence:

- The shares that both men and women bought subsequently underperformed and the shares they sold outperformed after they were sold.[1]

- Both men and women underperformed market and risk-adjusted benchmarks.[2]

- Those who traded the most performed the worst.[3]

- The more confident people were in their ability to either identify mispriced securities or time the market, the worse the results.[4]

- Men produced similar gross returns to women. However, men earned lower net returns as their greater turnover (trading activity) had a negative impact on results.[5]

- Single women produced better net returns than their married counterparts, presumably because they were not influenced by their overconfident spouses.[6]

- Demonstrating that more heads are not better than one, the average investment club lagged a broad market index by almost 4 per cent per year. Adjusting for risk, the performance was even worse. And clubs would have been better off never trading during the year.[7]

- Demonstrating that intelligence did not translate into higher returns, the Mensa (the high IQ society) Investment Club underperformed the S&P 500 Index by almost 13 per cent per year for 15 years.[8]

Exacerbating the problem is that investors are unaware of how poorly they are doing. A study on the subject found investors overestimated their own performance by an astounding 11.5 per cent a year. And the lower the returns, the worse investors were when judging their realised returns. While just 5 per cent believed they had experienced negative returns, the reality was that 25 per cent did so, and more than 75 per cent underperformed the relevant benchmark.[9]

Actively Managed Mutual Funds

The following is a brief summary of the evidence on the inability of actively managed funds to deliver outperformance:

- There has been no evidence of the ability to persistently generate outperformance beyond what would be randomly expected. The past performance of active managers is not a good predictor of the future.[10]

- Expenses reduced returns on a one-for-one basis (each pound spent reduced returns by approximately the same amount) and explained much of the persistent long-term underperformance of mutual funds.[11]

- Turnover reduced pre-tax returns by almost 1 per cent of the value of the trade.[12]

- In its own study, independent investment research firm Morningstar found that expense ratios were a better predictor than its star ratings. Simply ranking by expenses produced superior results — the lowest-cost funds tended to produce the highest returns.[13]

The bottom line is that the costs of share selection and market timing prove a difficult hurdle to overcome. And despite what most people believe, even long periods (such as 10 or even 15 years) of superior performance do not have predictive value: we cannot differentiate between skill and luck. One reason for this is that successful active management contains the seeds of its own destruction: the hurdles to generating alpha, or beating the market, increase as the amount of assets under management increase. This is an important contributor to the lack of persistent performance, even in the presence of skill.[14]

This body of evidence is likely what led Buffett to draw this conclusion:

"By periodically investing in an index fund the know–nothing investor can actually outperform most investment professionals."[15]

Pension Funds

It seems logical to believe that if anyone could beat the market, it would be corporate pension funds. Why is this a good assumption? Let's consider:

- Pension funds control large sums of money, giving them access to the best and brightest portfolio managers.

- They do not hire managers with a record of underperformance.

- Most pension funds hire professional consultants to help them perform due diligence in interviewing, screening and ultimately selecting the very best managers. These consultants employ armies of talented people who, you can be certain, have thought of every conceivable selection criteria.

- Their fees are much lower than the fees individual investors pay.

- Because pension funds benefit from favourable tax treatment, they do not have the same burden of taxes to pay that individuals must overcome.

Here's the evidence on the costs and perfor-mance of pension plans:

- In 2012, asset management costs (excluding per-formance fees and turnover costs) for the funds in which the Local Government Pension Scheme (i.e. public sector pensions) was invested amounted to £790 million — the vast majority going to active managers.

- Alternative investments (for example private equity and hedge funds), whilst helping diver-sify the investment, accounted for 40% of total fees yet only 10% of total assets.

- Using passive funds could have reduced man-agement fees by £230 million a year, with no loss in performance. Whilst *some* managers *had* outperformed, there was no evidence, *in aggregate*, that the Scheme had outperformed regional equity markets.

- This outcome reflected wider international evi-dence that any additional performance gener-ated by active investment managers cannot, on average, outweigh the additional costs of active management.[16]

Research in the US backs this up:

- Companies and their advisers hired investment managers who had outperformed. However, the outperformance didn't continue, as the post-hiring excess returns were indistinguishable from zero. If the funds had stayed with the fired investment managers, their returns would have been greater than those actually delivered by the newly hired managers.

- There was no evidence the number of managers beating their benchmarks was greater than pure chance.[17]

Studies on the performance of US corporate 401(k) plans (similar to UK personal pension plans) have found the same type of evidence: there is no ability to identify *ahead of time* the few active funds that will outperform their appropriate benchmarks.[18] As you can see, the evidence is overwhelming that passive investing is the winner's game. Active management is the loser's game because the odds of winning are so low that it is not prudent to try. In addition to the evidence, Nobel Laureate William Sharpe provided us with a simple and elegant proof of why active management must be, in aggregate, a loser's game.[19]

THE ARITHMETIC OF ACTIVE INVESTING

The market is made up of only two types of investors: active and passive. Assume that 70 per cent of investors are active and 30 per cent of investors are passive. Also assume the market returns 10 per cent.

On a pre-expense basis, passive investors must earn 10 per cent. What rate of return, before expenses, must the active managers, in aggregate, have earned? Because the sum of the parts must equal the whole, collectively, active managers must also have earned 10 per cent. The following equations show the maths where we need to work out the active investors' aggregate return (R) and:

- Total Market Return (T) = 10%

- Passive Investors' Market Share (P) = 10% × 30% = 3%

- Active Investors' Market Share (A) = R × 70% = 0.7R

We know that Total Market Return (T) = Passive Investors' Share (P) + Active Investors' Share (A); so: T = P + A. Now using basic algebra and substituting values from above:

- $10\% = 3\% + 0.7R$

- $0.7R = 10\% - 3\% = 7\%$

- $R = 7\%/0.7 = 10\%$

So the active investors' aggregate return is 10%.

It does not matter what percentages of market share you use, the outcome is the same, i.e. on a pre-expense basis the aggregate return for active managers is the same as the aggregate return for passive managers. The reason is that all equities must be owned by someone. If one active investor outperforms because he or she over-weighted the top-performing equities, another active investor must have underperformed by under-weighting those very same equities. In aggregate, on a pre-expense basis, active investors earn the same market rate of return as do passive investors. This holds true, no matter what asset class or type of market.

THE MATHS IS ALWAYS THE SAME

If, instead of using the total stock market, we substituted any other index or asset class, we would come to the same conclusion. That exposes the myth that active management works in "inefficient" asset classes like small-cap and emerging market stocks.

The same thing is true for bull and bear markets. If the market loses 10 per cent, the Vanguard FTSE UK Equity Index Fund will also lose 10 per cent on a pre-expense basis. In aggregate, so must active investors. The maths does not change for bull or bear markets.

So far, we have been discussing gross (before expenses) returns. Unfortunately, you do not earn gross returns; you earn returns net of expenses. To get to the net returns, the only kind you get to spend, we must subtract all costs:

- Expenses: the operating expenses of the fund

- Trading costs: the fund's costs of buying or selling securities

- Bid-offer spreads: the difference between the offer price (the price you pay when you buy) and the bid price (the price you receive when you sell)

- Brokerage commissions

- Market impact: the additional costs incurred while transacting large blocks of shares, resulting from changes in price before the full amount is bought or sold

- Cost of cash: the difference between the returns earned while sitting in cash and what would have been earned if fully invested.

Because active funds have higher expenses in each category, the cost of implementing a passive strategy will be less than that of an active one. Thus, in aggregate, passive investors must earn higher net returns than active investors. The mathematical facts cannot be denied. Active management is, in aggregate, a negative sum (loser's) game.

The evidence is overwhelming that the surest way to win the game of active management is to refuse to play. Thus, the winning strategy is to adopt a passive investment strategy. You can do that by investing in index mutual funds, such as those of Vanguard, Legal & General and HSBC. You can also consider investing in exchange-traded funds (ETFs) — such as iShares — which are essentially mutual funds that trade on exchanges throughout the day like shares.

Another option is passively managed funds (which though passive are not index funds) offered by fund families such as Dimensional Fund Advisers. Well-designed, passively managed, defined asset class funds can add value over similar index funds by maximising the benefits of indexing (such as low cost, broad diversification, low turnover and tax efficiency) while minimising some of the negatives (such as forced turnover which increases trading costs and creates tax inefficiencies).

Now that you know the right strategy, let's turn our attention to the development of a financial plan.

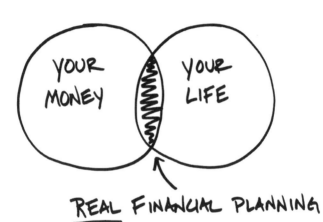

4

The Need to Plan: It is Not Only About Investments

Would you take a trip to a place you have never been without a road map, directions or a sat-nav? Would you start a business without spending lots of time and energy thoroughly researching that business and then writing a well-thought-out plan? The answers explain why the old and wise saying holds true: those who fail to plan, plan to fail.

Despite the wisdom of this statement, the vast majority of investors begin their investment journey without a plan, specifically, an investment policy statement (IPS) laying out the plan's objectives and the road map to achieving them. One reason so few investors have a well-developed, written and signed plan (what you should consider as a con-tract between you and yourself) is that the City and the media do not really want you to have one. The winning strategy for them is the losing strat-egy for you.

It is important to understand that a plan is nec-essary in order to be able to make rational decisions about investments. You cannot properly evalu-ate any investment without considering how the addition of that investment would impact the risk and return of your portfolio, and thus the odds of achieving the plan's objectives.

A Financial Plan Must Be a Living Document

Just as a business plan must be reviewed regularly to adapt to changing market conditions, an IPS and a financial plan must be living documents. If any of your plan's underlying assumptions change, the IPS should be altered to adapt to the change. Life-altering events (such as a birth or death in the family, a marriage or divorce, a large inheritance or a promotion or job loss) can affect the plan in dramatic ways. Thus, the IPS should be reviewed whenever a major life event occurs.

Market movements can also lead to changes in your assumptions. Bull markets may mean you're ahead of your goals, allowing you to take less risk. However, bull markets also lower expected future returns, meaning those still far from their goals may have to take more risk. (This does not mean you should take more risk. The alternative is to lower the goal.) The reverse is true of bear markets. A good policy is to review the IPS and its assumptions on an annual basis.

Before writing an IPS, you should thoroughly review your financial and personal status. You should consider not only your personal financial situation, but also such factors as:

- The stability of your job

- Whether the risk of your job is highly correlated with your share holdings

- Your investment horizon

- Your tolerance for risk

- The need for emergency reserves

Keep in mind that your investment horizon extends well beyond your planned retirement date;

it may even extend beyond your death if you are investing on behalf of your heirs.

You should also consider your need to take risk. Have you already saved enough? If so, why continue taking risk? Far too many investors fail to understand that the strategy to get rich (take risks) is entirely different from the strategy to stay rich (minimize risks, diversify the risks you take and don't spend too much).

It is also important to understand that it is not enough to have only a well-developed investment plan. It needs to be incorporated into an overall financial plan that also addresses estate and tax planning issues, as well as risk management issues such as the need for life, medical, and income protection insurance. It should also incorporate the onset of your state pension. Finally, your charitable intentions should be addressed.

A well-developed plan should also address such issues as objectives for transferring wealth to family members and ensuring they use it wisely according to your values. This can be incorporated into what is called a family wealth mission statement. You should consider having your children (and their spouses, if any) involved in your estate plan, including reading your will and understanding your intentions with respect to your property upon your death. They should also know the family's net worth. And they should get to know your advisers (your solicitor, accountant and financial adviser).

It is also important to develop a contingency plan in case your portfolio fails to deliver the returns that your plan anticipated. You should put in writing what actions you will take if a bear market leads to there being an unacceptable chance of your plan failing. You do not want to find yourself in a situation where your portfolio is likely to run out of assets or jeopardise an important legacy goal.

Your plan should list the specific actions. These actions might include delaying retirement or returning to the workforce, reducing current spending, reducing the financial goal, selling a home or moving to a location with a lower cost of living.

The written IPS should be combined with a financial plan that lists your specific goals, such as the amount you plan to add to your portfolio each year, the amount of assets you are trying to accumulate by a certain date, when you plan to begin withdrawals from the portfolio, and the amount in £s you plan on withdrawing each year. The required rate of return on your investment then needs to be calculated and a portfolio constructed that gives you the best chance of achieving this return whilst taking into account your ability and willingness to take risk. This will allow you to track progress toward the goal, making appropriate adjustments along the way.

The next step in developing your IPS is to specify your asset allocation, or the makeup of your portfolio. The IPS should include a formal asset allocation table identifying both the target allocation for each asset class and the rebalancing targets in the form of minimum and maximum tolerance boundaries. A written IPS serves as a signpost and helps provide the discipline needed to adhere to a strategy over time. Developing that asset allocation plan is the subject of the next chapter.

THE 5 BIG QUESTIONS:
① HOW MUCH CAN YOU SAVE?
② HOW MUCH RISK?
③ HOW MUCH WILL YOU NEED?
④ WHEN WILL YOU NEED IT?
⑤ WHAT DO YOU WANT TO LEAVE?

5

How Much Risk Should You Take? The Asset Allocation Decision

There's no one plan that's right for everybody. The amount of risk you should take and the makeup of your portfolio depends entirely on your unique ability, willingness and need to take risk. Let's begin with taking a look at the ability to take risk.

THE ABILITY TO TAKE RISK

The longer your investment horizon, the more risk you can take. This is because you have a greater ability to wait out a bear market. In addition, the longer the investment horizon, the more likely equities will provide higher returns than bonds. As a rule of thumb you could allocate up to 4 per cent of your portfolio to equities for each year of your investment horizon. The following table illustrates how this could work in helping you to divide your assets between riskier shares and safer bonds:

Investment Horizon	Maximum Equity Allocation (%)
0 – 4 years	0 to 10
5 years	20
10 years	40
15 years	60
25 years or longer	100

Besides your investment horizon, you should also consider your human capital. We can define human capital as the present value of potential future income derived from labour. It is an asset that does not appear on any balance sheet. It is also an asset that is not tradable like an equity or a bond. Thus, it is often ignored, at potentially great risk to the individual's financial goals. There are several important points to consider about your human capital.

First, when we are young, human capital is at its highest point. It is also often the largest asset individuals have when they are young. As we age and accumulate financial assets, and the time we have remaining in the workforce decreases, the amount of human capital relative to financial assets shrinks. This shift over time should be considered in terms of the asset allocation decision.

Second, we need to consider not only the magnitude of our human capital, but also its volatility. Some people (such as teachers and civil servants) have stable jobs. Their earned income is much like a bond. Other people (such as commission-only sales people, freelancers and building workers) have earned income that is more volatile and, thus, acts more like shares. Your asset allocation should incorporate these important points.

Third, you should consider the significance of human capital as a percentage of total assets. If human capital is a small percentage of the total portfolio (because there are large financial assets), the volatility of the human capital and its correlation to financial assets becomes less of an issue.

Fourth, to avoid having too many eggs in one basket, you should avoid investing in assets that have a high correlation with your human capital. Unfortunately, far too many people follow the advice of Peter Lynch, who managed Fidelity's Magellan Fund from 1977 to 1990, to "buy what you know". The result is that they invest heavily in the shares of their employers. This is a mistake on two fronts. The first is that it is a highly undiversified investment. The second is that the investment is likely to have a high correlation with the person's human capital. Employees of companies like Barings Bank and Lehman Brothers found out how costly a mistake that can be.

Fifth, human capital can be lost due to two risks that need to be addressed by means other than through investments. The first is the possibility of disability or an accident rendering you unable to work. This risk can be addressed by income protection insurance. The other risk is that of premature death. That issue can be addressed with life insurance. These issues highlight the importance of integrating your investment plan into an overall estate, tax and risk management plan.

There is one more important issue we need to consider about the ability to take risk — the need for liquidity. The need for liquidity is determined by the need for near-term cash requirements as well as the potential for unanticipated calls on capital.

A good rule of thumb is to have savings to cover six months of ordinary expenses.

THE WILLINGNESS TO TAKE RISK

The willingness to take risk is determined by what could be called the "strong stomach" test. Ask yourself this question: Can you stick with your investment strategy when markets crash? Successful investment management depends on your ability to withstand periods of stress and overcome the severe emotional hurdles present during bear markets like the ones experienced in 1973–74, 2000–02 and 2008. Thus, it is important not to take more risk than your stomach can handle. And besides, life is too short not to enjoy it.

The following table provides a guideline for you to consider. The maximum tolerable loss is independent of the time frame.

Maximum Tolerable Loss (%)	Maximum Equity Exposure (%)
10	20
20	40
30	60
40	80
50	100

THE NEED TO TAKE RISK

The need to take risk is determined by the rate of return required to achieve your financial objectives. The greater the rate of return needed, the more risk you need to take. However, you should also make sure you distinguish between real needs and desires. These are very personal decisions, with no right answers. However, the fewer things that fall into the needs column, the lower the need to take risk. Conversely, the more things that fall into the needs column, the more risk one will have to take.

THE MAKEUP OF THE PORTFOLIO

Once we have addressed the key issues of ability, willingness and need to take risk, we need to decide on the makeup of the portfolio. Volumes of research have found that the vast majority of the risk and expected return of your portfolio are determined by its asset allocation, meaning the percentage of your portfolio devoted to specific asset classes. More specifically, it is determined by the exposure to what are called risk factors. Riskier assets have higher *expected* (not guaranteed) returns. If the higher returns were guaranteed, there would be no risk. We begin our discussion with the broad category of equities.

Equities

In order of importance, the first decision is to determine how much of an allocation you will have to riskier shares versus bonds. Since shares are riskier than bonds, they provide greater *expected* returns.

The next decision involves dividing up your equity allocation among UK equities, international equities (the shares of other developed countries) and emerging-market equities. Within those three categories, you can divide your allocations further into small-cap shares or large-cap and value or growth.

Similar to the way shares have higher expected returns than bonds because they are riskier, small-cap and value shares have higher expected returns than their large-cap and growth counterparts. However, those higher expected returns come with additional risk. In other words, the higher expected returns of small-cap and value shares are not a free lunch; they are compensation for accepting incremental risk.

In addition to providing higher expected returns, small-cap and value stocks provide another benefit: they help to diversify your portfolio. The reason for this is that some of the risks of small-cap shares and of value shares are unique. Looking at the data series for each, we can see from their correlations of returns — the degree to which the historical returns of these asset classes vary together – that periods of time exist when, simply put, some asset classes (such as small and value stocks) zig while the markets zag.

The diversification benefits are very nicely illustrated in the lead up to and into the technology crash of the early 2000s:

- In 1998 the FTSE All Share returned almost 14 per cent, while UK smaller companies fell by almost 5 per cent and value stocks rose around 1 per cent.

- In 2000 the broad market fell by around 6 per cent, small-caps were flat and value stocks increased 10 per cent.

- During the peak-to-trough fall of the UK equity market from January 2000 to January 2003, the FTSE All Share Index was down around 43 per cent, and smaller companies fell 37 per cent, but value stocks fell by a much smaller 24 per cent.

Since no one has demonstrated the ability to determine ahead of time which asset class *will do well*, the winning strategy is to diversify your risks. Similar examples could be shown for international and emerging market stocks. The bottom line is that since diversification is the only free lunch in investing, you might as well eat a lot of it.

Bonds

Bonds have two risk factors: term (number of years to maturity) and default (credit). The longer the term to maturity and the lower the credit rating, the greater the risk and *expected* returns. So you need to decide how much you will allocate to high-quality versus lower-quality bonds, and how much you will allocate to short-term and intermediate-term bonds versus long-term bonds.

Before you tackle the type of bonds to own, it is critical that you understand the role bonds should play in a portfolio. The central role of bonds in a portfolio should be to dampen the risk of the overall portfolio to an acceptable level, which means you should minimise risks in your bond holdings. That makes the investment decision simple. A basic rule of thumb is to limit your holdings to the safest bonds: those that carry the full faith and credit of the Government, and which have maturities of less than five years (the 'maturity date' of a bond is the date at which the lenders – the investors – get repaid the principal sum due). If you choose to own corporate bonds (which entail more credit risk), the historical evidence suggests that you limit your holdings to those with remaining maturities of five years or less and focus on bonds that have investment-grade ratings – BBB or higher – indicating that the bond has a relatively low risk of default. Investors can find bond fund credit ratings and maturities on fund fact sheets. These guidelines simplify your decision.

Alternative Investments

The search for better performing investments typically leads investors to consider what are often called alternative investments. This term is generally used to describe investments beyond the familiar categories of shares and investment-grade bonds. The category includes such investments as property, commodities (for example precious metals, oil & gas, and wheat), private equity, venture capital, hedge funds, junk bonds, emerging market bonds, convertible bonds, preference shares and so-called structured investment products. A common element of alternative investments is that the City typically makes a lot of money as the purveyors of these products. The good news is that with the exception of property and commodities, the academic research demonstrates that you should not even consider owning any of the other alternatives. You certainly do not need them to develop a well-diversified portfolio or to achieve your goals.

The two alternatives worth considering are property and commodities. Property is a good diversifier of the risks of both shares and bonds. You can invest in property by owning an index fund (such as iShares, FTSE EPRA/NAREIT Developed Mkt, Property ETF or the BlackRock Global Property Securities Equity Tracker) that invests in a broad spectrum of publicly traded real estate investment trusts (REITs) – listed companies that invest in commercial, industrial and retail property primarily for rental income. Commodities serve a similar purpose, although robust product structures are quite limited for UK investors at present.

We now turn our attention to the tax wrapper decision, or the best places to hold your various investments for tax efficiency.

THE TAX WRAPPER DECISION

When faced with a choice of placing assets in either taxable or tax-advantaged accounts, taxable investors should first consider investing in tax advantageous accounts such as ISAs, Pension Plans and Offshore Investment Bonds. *You should, however, always remember to provide liquidity for unanticipated funding requirements* and you should not let the tax tail wag the dog.

Once you decide on your asset allocation you will need to also decide on whether you should invest in mutual funds or individual securities.

MUTUAL FUNDS OR INDIVIDUAL SECURITIES?

When implementing your plan, you will have to decide between investing in individual securities and using mutual funds (such as Unit Trusts, OEICs and SICAVs) and ETFs. To make the right choice, you need to be able to distinguish between two very different types of risk: good risk and bad risk. Good risk is the type you are compensated for taking. Risks that cannot be diversified away are called *systematic* risks: for example, you cannot diversify away the risks of investing in shares no matter how many you own. The compensation you receive for taking the risks comes in the form of greater *expected* returns.

On the other hand, bad risk is the type for which there is no such compensation. Thus, it is called *uncompensated* or *unsystematic* risk. One example of bad or uncompensated risk is the risk of the individual company (such as Northern Rock or Barings Bank). The risks of individual share ownership can be easily diversified away by owning index funds that basically own all the shares in an entire asset class/index. These vehicles eliminate the single-company risk in a low-cost and tax-efficient manner.

You can also diversify asset class risk by building a globally diversified portfolio, allocating funds across various asset classes: UK, international and emerging markets; large-cap and small-cap; value and growth; and property and commodities.

Because these risks can be diversified, the market does not compensate investors for taking such risks. The same is true of staying within a single asset class. This is why investing in individual companies and only one or a few asset classes has more in common with speculating than it does with investing. Investing means taking compensated risk. Speculating is taking uncompensated risk. Other examples of uncompensated risk are investing in sector funds (such as health care or technology) and individual country funds (other than a UK total stock market fund).

Prudent investors recognise the difference between speculating and investing. They take only risks for which they are compensated. Thus, when it comes to investing in risky assets, the only vehicles you should consider are low-cost mutual funds and ETFs. This advice applies to all risky assets, not just shares, but corporate bonds as well.

With bonds backed by the full faith and credit of the Government, the lack of credit risk means you can buy individual bonds and save the expense of a mutual fund. On the other hand, low-cost mutual funds and ETFs, in addition to providing the benefits of diversification, also provide the benefit of convenience, including, if you wish, the automatic reinvestment of income or, alternatively, using income for rebalancing. That benefit is at least worth considering.

We now turn to demonstrating the benefits of building a globally diversified portfolio.

THE THEORY OF DIVERSIFICATION

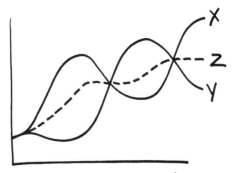

X = RISKY INVESTMENT #1
Y = RISKY INVESTMENT #2
Z = LESS RISKY "PORTFOLIO

6

How to Build a Well-Designed Portfolio

As we discussed in Chapter 5, diversification is the only free lunch in investing. Unfortunately, most investors fail to take advantage of this "all you can eat" opportunity because they do not build well-diversified portfolios. Instead, they hold a portfolio that consists of just a handful of equities. They do so because they make mistakes, such as being overconfident of their investment skills. They also tend to confuse the familiar with the safe, causing them to concentrate their holdings in companies they are familiar with, particularly the shares of their employer. This tendency typically results in minimal exposure to international equities.

Because most investors have not studied financial economics, read financial economic journals, or read books on modern portfolio theory, they do not have an understanding of how many equities are needed to build a truly diversified portfolio. To effectively diversify the risks of just the asset class of UK equities you would have to hold a minimum of around 50 equities. Once you expand your investment universe to include other developed markets equities and those of the emerging markets, it becomes obvious that the only way to effectively diversify a portfolio is through the use of mutual funds or ETFs.

However, even when individuals invest in mutual funds, they typically do not diversify effectively because they make the mistake of thinking that diversification is about the number of funds you own. Instead, it is about how well your investments are spread across different asset classes. For example, an investor who owns 10 different actively managed UK equity funds may believe that he is effectively diversified. While it is true that each fund will likely have some differentiation in its holdings from the others, it is possible that there will be considerable overlap resulting in a poorly diversified selection of equities. At the other end of the spectrum these 10 funds may result in the creation of an expensive "closet" index fund. The reason for this is that it is likely that the return of his portfolio, before expenses, will approximate the return of the FTSE All Share or similar index. After expenses, the odds are great it will underperform.

Even many individuals who invest in index funds get it wrong because they limit themselves to funds that mimic the FTSE All Share Index. At the very least, they should also include a significant allocation (perhaps 50 per cent or more of their share portfolio) to a fund such as an international equity fund or ETF. After all, the UK represents less than 10 per cent of the value of the global equity markets and less than 5 per cent of global GDP. Recent research also shows that over 85 per cent of all FTSE 350 revenues come from mining, energy and the financial services sector alone. Limiting your investments to only the UK results in minimal exposure to a whole range of other industries such as technology, software, electrical goods and car manufacturing.

MODERN PORTFOLIO THEORY AT WORK

The next step is to show you how simple it is to build a more effective, globally diversified portfolio. Many investors think that diversification means owning enough mutual funds. However, the key is spreading them across asset classes. After all, 10 different large-cap growth funds still means you only have exposure to one asset class.

We will begin with a portfolio that is 60 per cent allocated to UK equities and 40 per cent to low risk UK government bonds (i.e. gilts with a maturity of less than 5 years). The time frame will be the 39-year period, 1976–2014. This period was chosen because it is the longest for which we have data on all of the indexes we need. While maintaining the same 60 per cent equity/40 per cent bond allocation, we will then expand our investment universe to include other asset classes.

Step 1: We create a portfolio that consists of just two investments, the FTSE All Share Index for the UK equity allocation and the FTSE British Government Index (up to 5 years) for the lower risk bond portion. We will see how the portfolio performed if one had the patience to stay with this allocation from 1976 through to 2014 and rebalanced annually. We will then demonstrate how the portfolio's performance could have been made more efficient by increasing its diversification across asset classes. We do so in three more simple steps.

Portfolios are shown for illustrative purposes only. Indexes are not available for direct investment. Their performance does not reflect the expenses associated with the management of an actual portfolio, nor do indexes represent results of actual trading.

Portfolio A

FTSE All Share Index   60%

FTSE British Government Index (up to 5 years)   40%

1976–2014

	Annualised Return (%)	Annual Standard Deviation (%)	Ratio of return to risk (efficiency)
Portfolio A	11.2	10.4	1.1

By changing the composition of Portfolio A, we will see how we can improve the efficiency of our portfolio – increase the return relative to the amount of risk (volatility). To avoid being accused of data mining, we will alter our allocations by arbitrarily cutting the UK equity allocation in half, combining it with international equities.

Step 2: We begin by diversifying our equity holdings to include an allocation to international equities listed on the markets of other developed countries such as the US. Therefore, we reduce our allocation to the FTSE All Share Index from 60 to 30 per cent and allocate 30 per cent to the MSCI World ex-UK Index.

Portfolio B

FTSE All Share Index	30%
MSCI World ex-UK Index	30%
FTSE British Government index (up to 5 years)	40%

1976–2014

	Annualised Return (%)	Annual Standard Deviation (%)	Ratio of return to risk (efficiency)
Portfolio A	11.2	10.4	1.1
Portfolio B	10.7	9.1	1.2

The rate of return of the portfolio did fall by 0.5 per cent. That occurred because in this particular period the UK market provided higher returns than other global developed markets. Going forward there is no reason to expect this to continue to be the case. Basically, we should expect that developed markets should have the same returns over the long term. It is important to note that the reduction in volatility of the portfolio was 1.3 per cent, i.e. over twice the difference in returns, resulting in an improvement in the efficiency of the portfolio.

Step 3: Our next step is to reduce our UK allocation from 30 per cent to 20 per cent and add a 5 per cent allocation to both UK small and value stocks. The higher risk associated with these companies has in the past delivered, and is expected to deliver in the future, higher returns than the broad market. We do the same thing with our international allocation.

Portfolio C

FTSE All Share Index	20%
Dimensional UK Value Index	5%
Dimensional UK Small-Cap Index	5%
MSCI World ex-UK Index	20%
Dimensional International ex-UK Value Index	5%
Dimensional International ex-UK Small Index	5%
FTSE British Government Index (up to 5 years)	40%

1976–2014

	Annualised Return (%)	Annual Standard Deviation (%)	Ratio of return to risk (efficiency)
Portfolio A	11.2	10.4	1.1
Portfolio B	10.7	9.1	1.2
Portfolio C	11.4	9.2	1.2

The return of Portfolio C was 0.7 per cent higher than Portfolio B, while its volatility was only 0.1 per cent higher. The higher return is what we should expect as we added riskier small-cap and value stocks to our portfolio. The combined effect of the changes we made resulted in Portfolio C having a greater return than Portfolio A while also exhibiting 1.2 per cent less volatility.

Step 4: There is one more asset class we want to consider including in a portfolio – global commercial property, i.e. commercial, industrial and retail property investments around the world. These are represented by real estate investment trusts (REITs): companies listed on stock exchanges that invest in commercial property predominantly for rental income. This asset class can help to diversify some of the risks of investing in equities and bonds. Therefore, we will add a 10 per cent allocation to the

FTSE NAREIT Equity REITs TR Index, and reduce our allocations to UK and International equities accordingly.

Portfolio D

FTSE All Share Index	17%
Dimensional UK Value Index	4%
Dimensional UK Small-Cap Index	4%
MSCI World ex-UK Index	17%
Dimensional International ex-UK Value Index	4%
Dimensional International ex-UK Small Index	4%
FTSE NAREIT Equity REITs TR Index	10%
FTSE British Government Index (up to 5 years)	40%

1976–2014

	Annualised Return (%)	Annual Standard Deviation (%)	Ratio of return to risk (efficiency)
Portfolio A	11.2	10.4	1.1
Portfolio B	10.7	9.1	1.2
Portfolio C	11.4	9.2	1.2
Portfolio D	11.7	8.9	1.3

Some investors think of commercial property as a risky investment. However, you will note that its addition to the portfolio has not only reduced its volatility, but also increased the return, thus improving the "efficiency" of the portfolio. This "diversification benefit" is a reason to consider including an allocation to global commercial property in your portfolio.

The net result of all of our changes (from Portfolio A to Portfolio D) is that the portfolio's return increased 0.5 per cent and the volatility of the portfolio fell 1.5 per cent. The combination resulted in the risk ratio improving from 1.1 to 1.3, a relative increase of 18 per cent.

If you are wondering why there is no mention of emerging markets in any of the example portfolios, it is not because they are to be avoided: diversified portfolios *should* include exposure to emerging markets. The only reason they are not included here is because data on emerging markets only goes back to 1988 whereas our calculations cover a longer timeframe, going back to 1976.

You have now seen the power of modern portfolio theory at work. You saw how you can add risky (and, therefore, higher expected return) assets to a portfolio and reduce the risk of the portfolio whilst improving returns. That is the benefit of diversification.

LOOKING AT WORST CASE INVESTMENT HORIZONS

A useful way of looking at the benefit of spreading your investment risks amongst a number of asset classes can be clearly seen by looking at the worst case investment periods for Portfolios A to D during the same period. The longer term benefits are most interesting.

	Worst 1 year return per year %	Worst 5 year return per year %	Worst 10 year return per year %
Portfolio A	−18.0	−1.1	+2.3
Portfolio B	−15.9	−0.3	+2.1
Portfolio C	−17.1	+0.6	+3.0
Portfolio D	−17.1	+1.7	+3.5

Conclusion on diversifying your portfolio

Intuitively, few investors would baulk at the suggestion of spreading their investment eggs around a number of baskets. Some may be surprised at just how effective such an approach can be. Whilst at times of market turmoil all risky assets may fall together, your high quality bonds should provide strong downside protection. In addition, not all risky assets fall to the same degree and some recover faster than others.

PLAYING THE WINNER'S GAME

Through the step-by-step process described above, it becomes clear that one of the major criticisms of passive portfolio management – that it produces *average* returns – is wrong. There was nothing "average" about the returns of any of the diversified portfolios, and the results were achieved without any active management. Certainly the returns were greater than most of those of the average investor with a similar equity allocation, be it individual or institutional.

Passive investing delivers *market*, not average, returns. And it does so in a relatively low-cost manner. The average actively managed fund produces below market results and does so with great persistency.

By playing the winner's game of accepting market returns, you will almost certainly outperform the vast majority of both individual and institutional investors who choose to play the active game. There is only one caveat. You must learn to think of yourself akin to a postage stamp. The lowly postage stamp does only one thing, but it does it exceedingly well — it sticks to its letter until it reaches its destination. You must stick to your investment plan until you achieve your financial goals. Your only activities should be rebalancing, managing for taxes and adjusting the plan if the underlying assumptions change or you have any life-changing events. And that is the subject of our next chapter.

X

...SELL A LITTLE

...BUY A BIT

Y

[RE-BALANCE]

7

The Care and Maintenance of Your Portfolio

Just as a garden must undergo regular care and maintenance, regular maintenance must be performed on an investment portfolio. Otherwise, you will lose control over the most important determinant of risk and returns: your portfolio's asset allocation. That makes rebalancing one of the two important items on the portfolio maintenance agenda. The other is tax management. We will discuss both, beginning with rebalancing.

REBALANCING

Rebalancing restores the portfolio to your desired risk profile, the one you wrote in your IPS. Without regularly rebalancing a portfolio, you will find that the "risk profile" of your portfolio will change. In rising markets, your portfolio will become more aggressive as your equity holdings become a bigger percentage of your portfolio. Without rebalancing, your equity allocation will typically be increasing when valuations are higher and, thus, expected returns are lower. In falling markets, the reverse is true. Your equity allocation will typically be decreasing when valuations are lower and, thus, expected returns are higher. That does not sound like an intelligent approach.

Buy Low and Sell High

The rebalancing process is simple, though not easy. This is because emotions can get in the way. Rebalancing allows you to reduce your allocation in the asset classes that performed relatively the best (selling high) and increase the position in the asset classes that performed relatively poorly (buying low). Isn't it every investor's dream to buy low and sell high?

Another benefit of rebalancing is that over time it will produce a bonus — the portfolio's annualised return will exceed the *weighted average* of the annualised returns of the component asset classes. This is referred to as a *diversification return*, or "rebalancing bonus". And the more volatile the asset classes are within the portfolio, and the lower their correlations, the greater the effect of rebalancing. The reason is that when you rebalance you will be buying at lower lows and selling at higher highs.

An important decision to make is how to determine the rebalancing parameters. The following will provide you with a reasonable rule of thumb to consider.

The 5/25 Per Cent Rule

Rebalancing may cause transaction fees to be incurred, and it may also have tax implications. Therefore, it should be done only whenever new funds are available for investment or when your asset allocation has shifted substantially out of alignment. A reasonable rule of thumb is to use a 5/25 per cent rule in an asset class's allocation before rebalancing. That is, rebalancing should occur only if the change in an asset class's allocation is greater than either an absolute 5 percentage points or 25 per cent of the original target allocation, whichever is less.

For example, let's assume an asset class was given an allocation of 10 per cent of the portfolio. Applying the 5 per cent rule, one would not rebalance unless that asset class's allocation had either risen to 15 per cent or fallen to 5 per cent. However, using the 25 per cent rule one would reallocate if it had risen or fallen by just 2.5 per cent to either 12.5 or 7.5 per cent.

In this case, the 25 per cent figure was the governing factor. If one had a 50 per cent asset-class allocation, the 5/25 per cent rule would cause the 5 per cent figure to be the governing factor since 5 per cent is less than 25 per cent of 50 per cent, which is 12.5 per cent. In other words, one rebalances if either the 5 per cent or the 25 per cent test indicates the need to do so.

While rebalancing should be done based on risk (as described above), not on the calendar, if you are doing it yourself keep it simple and apply the 5/25 per cent test at least annually. You should be sure that the test is applied at all three levels:

- The broad level of equities and bonds

- The level of domestic and international asset classes

- The more narrowly defined individual asset class level (such as emerging markets, property, small-cap, value, and so on).

For example, suppose one had six equity asset classes, each with an allocation of 10 per cent, resulting in an equity allocation of 60 per cent. If each equity class appreciated so that it then constituted 11 per cent of the portfolio, no rebalancing would be required if you only looked at the individual asset-class level (the 5/25 per cent rule was not triggered). However, looking at the broader equity class level, we see that rebalancing is required. With six equity asset classes, each constituting 11 per cent of the portfolio, the equity asset class as a whole is now at 66 per cent. The increase from 60 to 66 per cent triggers the 5/25 per cent rule. The reverse situation may occur where the broad asset classes remain within guidelines but the individual classes do not. Once again, just as with the model portfolios, the 5/25 per cent test is just a guideline. You can create your own guideline for rebalancing for risk. The discipline the process provides is more important than the percentages you choose.

The IPS Asset Allocation and Rebalancing Table

Your Investment Policy Statement (IPS) should include an asset allocation and rebalancing table (example opposite). The table should include both the target levels for each asset class and the minimum and maximum levels to which the allocations will be allowed to drift. Some drift should be allowed to occur, because rebalancing generally involves costs, including transaction fees and taxes in taxable accounts.

The Rebalancing Process

In the accumulation phase, there are two ways to rebalance. The first is to sell what has done relatively well in order to buy what has done relatively poorly. The second is to use new cash to raise the allocations of the asset classes that are below targeted levels. A combination of the two strategies can be used. Utilising new cash is preferred; it reduces transaction costs, and it reduces or eliminates the capital gains that are generated when selling appreciated assets in taxable accounts. In the withdrawal phase, investors can sell what has done relatively well.

Sample Rebalancing Table Using 5/25 Rule

Asset Class	Minimum Allocation (%)	Target Allocation (%)	Maximum Allocation (%)
FTSE All Share Index	15.00	20.00	25.00
Dimensional UK Value Index	3.75	5.00	6.25
Dimensional UK Small-cap Index	3.75	5.00	6.25
MSCI World ex-UK Index	15.00	20.00	25.00
Dimensional International ex-UK Value Index	3.75	5.00	6.25
Dimensional International ex-UK Small Index	3.75	5.00	6.25
FTSE NAREIT Equity REITs TR Index	9.00	12.00	15.00
Total Equities	**65.00**	**70.00**	**75.00**
FTSE British Government Index (up to 5 years)	25.00	30.00	35.00
Total Bonds	**25.00**	**30.00**	**35.00**

A strategy to consider is to have distributions paid in cash, rather than automatically reinvested, and use the cash to rebalance. However, you should consider the size of the portfolio and any transaction costs that might be incurred. For small accounts where transaction costs are present, this might not be a good strategy. Here are some other recommendations on the rebalancing process:

- Consider if incremental funds will become available in the near future (such as a tax refund, a performance bonus, proceeds from a sale, or dividends). If capital gains taxes will be generated by rebalancing, it might be prudent to wait until the new cash is available.

- Consider delaying rebalancing if it generates significant taxable capital gains. Also consider how long it will be before additional funds can be generated to rebalance.

- If significant capital gains taxes are generated, consider rebalancing to only the minimum/maximum tolerance ranges rather than restoring allocations to the target levels.

We now turn to the other important maintenance item, tax management.

TAX MANAGEMENT

While the winning strategy is to use a passive investment strategy, passively managing the taxable portion of the portfolio without regard to taxes is a mistake. An investor can improve the after-tax returns of a portfolio by proactive tax management. Tax management involves the following actions:

- Choose the most tax-efficient vehicles.

- Use your annual ISA and pensions allowances.

- Use your annual Capital Gains Tax allowances

- Realise losses to offset gains, thus reducing any potential capital gains tax liability.

Remember, just because an opportunity – for example investing in films or Venture Capital Trusts (VCTs) – is presented as a tax break, it doesn't necessarily mean it is a good investment. As mentioned in Chapter 5, be sure not to let the tax tail wag the dog.

We next turn to the question of whether you should be a do-it-yourself investor or hire an adviser.

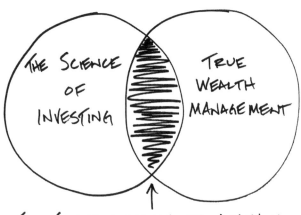

THE SCIENCE OF INVESTING

TRUE WEALTH MANAGEMENT

THE GREATEST CHANCE OF ACHIEVING YOUR FINANCIAL AND LIFE GOALS

8

Should You Hire a Financial Adviser?

Whether we are talking about home repairs or investing, individuals can be categorised into two broad groups: those who hire professionals and the "do-it-yourselfers" — those who do not want to pay professionals for something they believe they can do just as well. Of course, some who belong to the do-it-yourself group would be better off hiring professionals. One reason is that if something is not done right the first time, the cost of correcting errors can far exceed the cost of a professional to do it right in the first place. Another is that while you can recover from making a mistake while trying to fix a leaky tap, the damage done by financial errors can take years to recover from, and can even be irreversible.

If you are considering being a do-it-yourself investor, ask yourself the following five questions:

1. Do I have all the knowledge needed to develop an investment plan, integrate it into an overall estate, tax and risk management (insurance of all types) plan, and then provide the ongoing care and maintenance that is required?

2. Do I have the mathematical skills needed? Investing requires a knowledge that is more than just simple arithmetic. In addition, a familiarity with probability theory and statistics such as correlations of various moments of distribution (for example skewness and kurtosis) would be useful.

3. Do I have the ability to determine the appropriate asset allocation, one that provides the greatest odds of achieving my financial goals while not taking more risk than I have the ability and willingness to take? An important part of the planning process includes cash flow modelling, where you

look at alternative scenarios and the range of possible outcomes depending on assumptions made.

4. Do I have a strong knowledge of financial history? You should be aware of how often shares have provided negative returns, how long bear markets have lasted, and how deep they have been. Those who do not know their history are likely to repeat past mistakes.

5. Do I have the temperament and the emotional discipline needed to adhere to a plan in the face of the many crises I will almost certainly face? Are you confident that you have the fortitude to withstand a severe drop in the value of your portfolio without panicking? Will you be able to rebalance back to your target allocations (keeping your head while most others are losing theirs), buying more shares when the light at the end of the tunnel seems to be a train coming the other way? Think back to how you felt and acted after the events of September 11, 2001 and during the financial crisis that began in 2007.

Experience demonstrates that fear often leads to paralysis, or even worse, panicked selling and the abandonment of well-developed plans. When subjected to the pain of a bear market, even knowledgeable investors, who know what to do, fail to do the right thing because they allow emotions to take over, overriding what their brain knows is the correct action to take. This results in what Carl Richards calls "the behaviour gap". The term is used to describe the failure of investors to earn the same return as that earned by the very funds in which they invest. Ask yourself: Have I always done the right thing? Have my returns matched those of my investments?

If you have passed this test, you are part of a small minority. This book provides you with not only the winning strategy of broad global diversification and passive investing, but also guidance on how to construct a portfolio to address your unique circumstances. And the book's conclusion contains my list of the 30 Rules of Prudent Investing that will help you achieve your goals. If you are interested in learning more about how to develop an overall financial plan that is tailored to your unique situation, read *The Only Guide You'll Ever Need for the Right Financial Plan.*

Alternatively, you may recognise that you do not have the knowledge, temperament or the discipline to succeed on your own. And even if you decide that you meet these requirements, you may recognise that a good financial adviser can add value in many ways, including freeing you to focus your attention on the most important things in your life such as time spent with family, friends, or meaningful endeavours. Thus, you may place a greater value on that time than the cost spent on advice. It is a choice about finding the right balance in your life.

If you decide to hire a financial adviser, that choice will be one of the most important decisions you will ever make, because it will have the greatest impact. Thus, it is critical that you get it right. Here is valuable advice: there are three criteria that should be absolutes when searching for the right adviser. These criteria are:

* A fiduciary standard of care;

* Advice based on science (evidence from peer reviewed journals), not opinions;

- Investment planning that has been integrated into an overall financial plan.

A FIDUCIARY STANDARD OF CARE

There are several things you can do in your due diligence to give you the best chance to receive unbiased advice. First, choose an independent financial adviser who operates on a fee-only basis.

Second, you need to make sure that all potential conflicts of interest are fully disclosed. Along with asking questions, you should review the firm's entry in the Financial Services Register on the Financial Conduct Authority (FCA)'s website, the qualifications of the firm's advisers and its investment strategy. Careful due diligence helps minimise the risk of an expensive mistake.

Third, you should require that the firm's advisers invest their personal assets (including the firm's profit-sharing and/or retirement plan) based on the same set of investment principles and in the same or comparable securities that they recommend to their clients. While you should expect to see different asset allocations than those being recommended to you (as each investor has his own unique circumstances), the investment vehicles should be the same.

EVIDENCE-BASED ADVICE

You should consider working only with a firm whose investment strategy and advice is based on the science of investing, not on opinions. To demonstrate the wisdom of this advice, consider the following situation. You are not feeling well. You make an appointment to visit a doctor your friend has recommended. The doctor's job is to diagnose the problem and recommend treatment. After a thorough exam, he turns around to his bookshelf and reaches for the latest copy of *Men's Health* magazine carrying the headline *'Detox in 10 minutes'*. Before hearing his advice you are probably already thinking it is time to get a second opinion. Therefore, you make an appointment with another doctor. After her examination, she reaches for a copy of the *British Medical Journal (BMJ)*. At this point, you are feeling much better about the advice you are about to receive. The financial equivalent of the *BMJ* is a publication such as *The Journal of Finance* (bedtime reading only for those truly interested in the science of investing). The advisory firm should be able to cite evidence from peer-reviewed journals supporting their recommendations. You should not be acting solely on advice taken from the equivalents of *Men's Health* — such as *Moneyweek* or *Investors Chronicle.*

INTEGRATED FINANCIAL PLANNING

Because plans can fail for reasons that have nothing to do with an investment plan, it is critical that the firm you choose will integrate an investment plan into an overall estate, tax and risk management plan.

A well-developed financial plan includes a detailed analysis of the need for:

- Life insurance, for replacing income, paying estate taxes and/or transferring wealth to heirs or a charity

- Income Protection insurance, in case you can't work

- A lifetime annuity to cover the risk of running out of money because you live longer than expected

- A long-term care plan, to protect against care costs draining your assets

- Property and vehicle insurance, such as for homes, cars and boats, and against fire and floods

- Personal liability insurance, including an umbrella (excess liability) policy.

It is important to understand that plans can fail even when estate planning is done well. For example, far too often individuals pay for costly solicitors to develop well-thought-out estate plans only to have the trusts created either go totally unfunded, or be funded with the wrong type of assets.

Estate plans can also derail you because the beneficiaries have not been properly named (resulting from a failure to update documents to address life events such as divorce or death) or because the type or method of asset distribution is inappropriate (for instance, directing assets to be distributed directly to a beneficiary with demonstrated creditor, bankruptcy or financial management issues). This is another example of why a financial plan must be a living document, one that is reviewed on a regular basis.

It is also critical to understand that estate plans can fail despite the best efforts of top-notch professional advisers. Unfortunately, it is not uncommon for estates to lose their assets and family harmony following the transition of the estate. This occurs because beneficiaries are unprepared, they do not trust one another, and communication breaks down. While great attention is typically paid to preparing the *assets* for transition to the beneficiaries, very little, if any, attention is being paid to preparing the *beneficiaries* for the assets they will inherit. A good advisory firm can add great value by helping to prepare and educate beneficiaries for the wealth they will inherit.

There are many other ways a good financial advisory firm can and should add value. The following is a partial list.

- Retirement planning, including cash withdrawal strategies. Choosing the most efficient amount and account from which assets should be withdrawn as the sequencing can make a big difference in after-tax results. Another critically important decision is when to begin taking your state pension.

- Regular, ongoing communications, especially during times of crisis. Education protects you from having your emotions take control of your portfolio.

- Ongoing education about innovations in finance. The knowledge of how markets work advances on a persistent basis. Thus, you should be sure that the firm has the depth of resources to stay on top of the latest research.

- The ability to analyse complex financial products, helping you avoid purchasing costly products that are meant to be sold, not bought.

- Disciplined cost- and tax-effective rebalancing and tax management that is not driven by the calendar, but by how the portfolio's assets are performing.

- Advice on how best to cover the costs of further education.

- Selecting investments for personal and employer defined contribution pension plans.

- Gifting to heirs and charities in the most effective manner.

- Home purchase and mortgage financing decisions.

- The management and ultimate disposition of large concentrated positions with low-cost basis (typically shares in your employer or equities that have been inherited).

- Ongoing performance tracking, measuring the progress versus your plan and recommending adjustments that are necessary to prevent failure.

- Acting as an "insurance policy" in the event of a death of a family member who is responsible for managing financial matters.

Clearly, no one adviser can be an expert in all of these areas. Therefore, when choosing a firm be sure that it has a team of experts that can help address each of these areas. You should also make sure that the firm's comprehensive wealth management services are provided by registered individuals who have Chartered or Certified Financial Planner (CFP™) status. Note that the internationally-recognised CFP™ credential is granted to advisers who have demonstrated their expertise in personal financial planning. And once the designation is granted, it must be maintained through continuous professional development to keep it current.

It is also important to be clear that the firm will deliver a high level of personal attention and develop strong personal relationships. This should be part of your due diligence process as you check the firm's reputation with other local professionals (such as accountants and solicitors) and client references.

Another part of your investigation should be asking the adviser how he or she spends time at work. You might ask: "Can you please tell me about your average day?" What you are looking for is an adviser who spends the majority of their time solving their client's concerns about such issues as:

- Making smart decisions about money.

- Minimising income, gift and estate taxes.

- Transferring assets to the next generation.

- Protection from third parties unjustifiably taking their assets.

- Interest in making significant charitable gifts.

Your investigation should include sharing all of your concerns with the adviser. The objective is to develop a deep understanding of how the adviser can help you address these concerns and ensure that you are confident you have a high level of trust in the adviser, his/her support team, and the advisory firm as a whole.

There is one last point we need to cover. As is the case with the choice of investment vehicles, costs matter. But what really matters is the value added relative to the cost. The lowest cost investment vehicle may not be the best choice. Remember that while good advice doesn't have to be expensive, bad advice almost always will cost you dearly, no matter how little you pay for it.

The choice of a financial adviser is one of the most important decisions you will ever make. That is why it is so important to perform a thorough due diligence. The bottom line is that you want to be sure that the firm you choose is one where the science of investing meets true wealth management, and that the services are delivered in a highly personal manner.

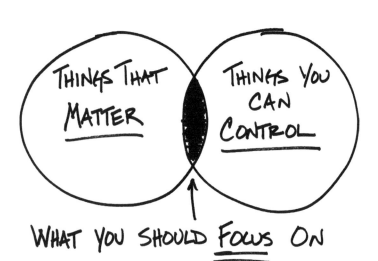

9

Winning the Game of Life

As we discussed in Chapter 3, there is an overwhelming body of evidence demonstrating that passive investing is the prudent investment strategy. Passive investing also allows you to win the far more important game: the game of life. The following tale demonstrates the wisdom of that statement.

An expert in time management was invited to speak to an MBA class. After a brief introduction she reached down and produced a very large jar and set it on a table in front of her. She then reached down again and produced a box filled with big rocks. She proceeded to remove the rocks from the box and carefully placed them, one at a time, into the jar. When no more rocks would fit inside the jar, she asked the class, "Is this jar full?"

Everyone yelled, "Yes." She then reached under the table, pulled out a bucket of gravel, dumped some in, and shook the jar. This caused pieces of gravel to work themselves down into the spaces between the big rocks. She continued this process until no more gravel could be placed into the jar. She then asked the class, "Is the jar full?" One student, getting the idea, answered, "No." She then reached under the table, brought out a bucket of sand, and started dumping the sand into the jar. The sand began to fill the spaces between the rocks and the gravel. She continued until no more sand could fit into the jar. Once more she asked, "Is this jar full?" This time everyone shouted, "No!" She then grabbed a jug of beer and poured until the jar was filled to the brim. She then asked the class, "What is the moral of the story?" An eager student raised his hand and said, "The moral of the story is that no matter how full your schedule is, there's always time for a couple of beers!"

The speaker replied, "Nice try, but that is not the moral of the story. The truth this illustration teaches us is that if you do not put the big rocks in first, you can never get them in." To each of us, the "big rocks" mean something different, but at the core, the big rocks are those things that provide the richest meaning to our lives.

As a passive investor when I come home from my busy day, I get to sit down with a glass of wine and ask my wife about her day and how my kids and grandchildren are doing. Because I did not spend my time trying to beat the market, I also got to coach my youngest daughter's softball, soccer and basketball teams. I also read about 70 books each year, do community service, play tennis, and focus on the other big rocks, the really important things in my life.

Investors following an active management strategy spend much of their precious leisure time watching the latest business news, studying the latest charts, reading financial trade publications, and so on. What they are really doing is focusing on the gravel, the sand, and the water. Therefore, even if they are among the very few who are successful at the game of active investing, the "price" of success may be that they lose the far more important game of life.

The question for you to consider is: What are the big rocks in your life? Is the big rock in your life trying to generate extra returns through active management strategies that require you to "invest" large amounts of your time? Or are the big rocks in your life time spent with your loved ones, your faith, your education, your dreams, a worthy cause, or teaching or mentoring others? If you do not already know the answer, perhaps this story will help you find it.

Shortly after my first book was published in 1998, I received a call from a doctor. He had been in practice just a few years. He had a wife and a young child, with another on the way. He had become caught up in the euphoria of the bull market and the advent of day trading. He had seen many of his doctor friends generate large profits from trading shares and he thought he should get in on this easy money.

After putting in his typical long day he would head straight for his computer and the Internet. He spent hours studying charts and investment reports and following the chat boards. Within a few months he had turned his small investment stake into about $100,000. Unfortunately, his wife no longer had a husband, and his child no longer had a father. He was now married to his investments. His wife began to seriously question their marriage. *Luckily*, within a few months he had lost all his profits.

Fortunately, the doctor realised that his original gains were likely a matter of luck and that he had been a beneficiary of a bull market. More important, he recognised that he was not paying attention to his family. When discussing this with a friend, his friend suggested that he read *The Only Guide to a Winning Investment Strategy You'll Ever Need*. After doing so he called to thank me for helping him find the winner's game in investing, but more importantly for helping him find the winner's game in life. From then on he knew to focus on the big rocks in his life.

The following is another true story. About one year after my first book was published I met Rick Hill. Rick was a sophisticated investor with an MBA from Wharton, University of Pennsylvania. Rick had about 30 years of experience in financial management. After meeting with one of my partners, and having read my book, Rick became a client. Eventually, Rick joined Buckingham Asset Management as a financial adviser so that he could help others enjoy the benefits of passive investing. Upon joining he related this story.

Rick told me that he used to spend many hours every day reading financial publications, researching stocks, and watching the financial news. And this was after spending a long day at the office. After adopting the principles of modern portfolio theory, the efficient markets hypothesis, and passive investing he found that he no longer needed to do those things. He recognised that he had been paying attention to what was nothing more than noise and that it only distracted him from the winner's game.

Rick and his wife sat down and calculated that by adopting a passive investment approach he had actually recaptured six weeks per year of his life! It is one thing to spend six weeks a year in productive activities. However, Rick had realised that the activities in which he was engaged were counterproductive because of the expenses and taxes incurred when he was implementing an active strategy. And, that didn't include placing a value on the most precious resource he had, time. He only had a limited amount of it, and did not want to spend it on less than optimal activities.

INVESTING
DONE
RIGHT

WATCHING
GRASS
GROW

BOTH ARE BORING !

Conclusion

I became the director of research for BAM Advisor Services because I wanted to teach investors the knowledge necessary to make prudent investment decisions. Through my writings and interactions with investors, I believe I have accomplished that objective—though there is a lot more work to do.

The greatest pleasure I have received from my efforts is that many readers have told me that the greatest value they received from my books is that the quality of their lives has been improved. Armed with the knowledge of how markets work, and with a well-developed financial plan tailored to their unique situation, they are able to ignore the noise of the market and the investment pandering of Wall Street, and focus on the "big rocks" in their lives.

I shared with you the benefits of indexing and passive investing because I feel they provide the most prudent solution for all investors. It is how you receive market returns in a low-cost and tax-efficient manner, providing you with the greatest likelihood of achieving your goals. Adopting this approach also frees you from combing through financial publications, allowing you to spend your precious free time in meaningful activities with those you love, thus enriching your life.

Finally, it is important to remember that despite what the City and the financial press want you to believe, investing was never meant to be exciting. Instead, it is about achieving your financial goals with the least amount of risk. To give yourself the best chance of achieving that objective, be sure to follow my 30 Rules of Prudent Investing.

30 Rules of
Prudent Investing

W̶hile we search for the answers to the complex problem of how to live a longer life, there are simple solutions that can have a dramatic impact. For example, it would be hard to find better advice on living longer than do not smoke, drink alcohol in moderation, eat a balanced diet, get at least half an hour of aerobic exercise three to four times a week, and belt up before driving. The idea that complex problems can have simple solutions is not limited to the question of living a longer life.

I have spent almost 40 years managing financial risks for two financial institutions as well as advising individuals and multinational corporations on the management of financial risks. Based on those experiences, I have compiled a list of rules that will give you the greatest chance of achieving your financial goals.

1. **Do not take more risk than you have the ability, willingness, or need to take**. Plans fail because investors take excessive risks. The risks show up unexpectedly, which leads to the abandonment of plans. When developing your plan, consider your horizon, stability of income, ability to tolerate losses and the rate of return required to meet your goals.

2. **Never invest in any security unless you fully understand the nature of all of the risks**. If you cannot explain the risks to your friends, you should not invest. Fortunes have been lost because people did not understand the type of risks they were taking.

3. **The more complex the investment, the faster you should run away**. Complex products are designed to be sold, not bought. You can be sure the complexity is designed in favour of the issuer, not the investor. Investment bankers do not play Santa Claus

and hand over higher returns because they like you.

4. **Risk and return are not necessarily related; risk and *expected* return are related**. If there were no risk, there would not be higher expected returns.

5. **If the security has a high yield, you can be sure the risks are high even if you cannot see them**. The high yield is like the shiny apple with which the evil queen entices Snow White. Investors should never confuse yield with expected return. Snow White could not see the poison inside the apple. Similarly, investment risks may be hidden, but you can be sure they are there.

6. **A well-designed plan is necessary for successful investing, but you must also have the discipline to stay the course, rebalance and manage tax as needed**. Unfortunately, most investors have no written plan. And emotions such as greed and envy in bull markets and fear and panic in bear markets can cause even well-designed plans to be discarded.

7. **Investment plans must be integrated into well-designed estate, tax and risk management (insurance of all kinds) plans**. The best investment plans can fail because of events unrelated to financial markets. For example, the breadwinner dies without sufficient life insurance, or suffers an accident or becomes ill, and has insufficient income protection or health insurance in place.

8. **Do not treat the highly improbable as impossible, or the highly likely as certain**. Investors assume that if their horizon is long enough, there is little to no risk. The result is they take too much risk. Taking too much risk causes investors with long horizons to become short-term investors. Shares are risky no matter the horizon. And remember, just because something has not happened, doesn't mean it cannot or will not.

9. **The consequences of decisions should dominate the probability of outcomes**. We buy insurance against low probability

events (such as death) when the consequences of not having the insurance can be
too great. Similarly, investors should insure
their portfolios (by having an appropriate
amount of high-quality bonds) against low
probability events when the consequences
of not doing so can be too great to even con-
template, let alone accept.

10. **The strategy to get rich is entirely different from the strategy to stay rich.**
One gets rich by taking risks (or inheriting
the assets). One stays rich by minimising
risks, diversifying and not spending too
much.

11. **The only thing worse than having to
pay taxes is not having to pay them**.
The "too many eggs in one basket" problem
often results from holding a large amount of
shares with a low cost basis. Large fortunes
have been lost because of the refusal to pay
taxes.

12. **The safest port in a sea of uncertainty is
diversification**. Portfolios should include
appropriate allocations to the asset classes

of large-cap and small-cap, value and growth, property, international developed markets, emerging markets, commodities and high quality, low volatility bonds.

13. **Diversification is always working; sometimes you'll like the results and sometimes you won't.** Once you diversify beyond popular indexes (such as the FTSE 100 or FTSE All-Share), you will be faced with periods when a popular benchmark index outperforms your portfolio. The noise of the media will test your ability to adhere to your strategy.

14. **The prices of all equities and risky bond assets (such as high-yield bonds and emerging market bonds) tend to fall during financial crises**. Your plan must account for this.

15. **It isn't enough to find mispriced securities. You have to make money after accounting for the costs**. The history books are filled with investors who tried to exploit "mispricings", only to find that the costs exceeded any benefits.

16. **Investing in shares is a positive sum game; expenses make outperforming the market a negative sum game**. Risk-averse investors do not play negative sum games. And most investors are risk averse. Use only low-cost, passively managed investments and take full advantage of tax allowances and appropriate tax efficient investment vehicles.

17. **Owning individual shares and sector funds is more akin to speculating than investing**. The market compensates investors for risks that cannot be diversified away, like the risk of investing in equities versus bonds. Investors shouldn't expect compensation for diversifiable risk — the unique risks related to owning shares in just one company. Prudent investors accept risk only for situations in which they will be compensated with higher expected returns.

18. **Take your risks with shares**. The role of bonds is to provide the anchor to the portfolio, reducing overall portfolio risk to the appropriate level.

19. **Before acting on seemingly valuable information, ask yourself why you believe that information is not already incorporated into prices**. Only *incremental* insight has value. Capturing *incremental* insight is difficult because there are so many smart, highly motivated analysts doing the same research. If you hear recommendations from your broker or read them in the financial pages, the market already knows the information it is based on. It has already been incorporated into prices and has no value.

20. **The five most dangerous investment words are "This time, it is different."** Getting caught up in the mania of the "new thing" is why "the surest way to create a small fortune is to start out with a large one" is a cliché.

21. **The market can remain irrational longer than you can remain solvent**. Bubbles do occur. However, while they eventually burst, they can grow larger and last longer than your resources.

22. **If it sounds too good to be true, it is.** When money meets experience, the experience gets the money and the money gets the experience. The only free lunch in investing is diversification.

23. **Never work with a commission-based investment adviser.** Commissions create the potential for biased advice.

24. **Only work with fee-based advisers who will provide a fiduciary standard of care**. That is the best way to be sure the advice provided is in your best interest. There is no reason not to insist on a fiduciary standard.

25. **Separate the services of financial adviser, fund manager, custodian and trustee, and understand who each of these parties are**. This minimises the risk of fraud.

26. **Since we live in a world of cloudy crystal balls, a strategy is either right or wrong before we know the outcome**. In general, lucky fools do not have any idea they are lucky. Even well-designed plans

can fail, because risks that were accepted occur. And risks that were avoided, because the consequences of their materialising would be too great to accept, may not occur.

27. **Hope is not an investment strategy**. Base your decisions on the evidence from peer-reviewed academic journals.

28. **Keep a diary of your predictions about the market**. After a while, you will conclude that you should not act on your "insights".

29. **There is nothing new in investing, just the investment history you do not know**. The knowledge of financial history will enable you to anticipate risks and incorporate them into your plan.

30. **Good advice does not have to be expensive; but bad advice always costs you dearly, no matter how little you pay for it**. Smart people do not choose the cheapest dentist or the cheapest accountant. Costs matter — but it is the value added relative to the cost of the advice that ultimately is most important.

The following is not only the most important message in the book, but is a fitting ending: While it is a tragedy that the vast majority of investors unnecessarily miss out on market returns that are available to anyone adopting a passive investment strategy, the truly great tragedy is that they also miss out on the important things in life in pursuit of what I call the "Holy Grail of Outperformance". My fondest wish is that this book has led you to the winner's game in both investing and, far more important, life.

Notes

Foreword

1. The Investment Association statistics on authorised investment funds 2014: http://www.theinvestmentassociation.org/media-centre/press-releases/2015/press-release-statistics1014.html

2. *Morningstar* 16.01.15 http://www.thinkadvisor.com/2015/01/16/investors-embraced-passive-funds-eschewed-active-m

A few words about Warren Buffett

1. *Forbes* The World's Billionaires real-time ranking on 17.03.15 http://www.forbes.com/profile/warren-buffett/

2. "My philanthropic pledge" http://money.cnn. com/2010/06/15/news/newsmakers/Warren_ Buffett_Pledge_Letter.fortune/

3. http://refspace.com/quotes/Warren_Buffett/ investment

4. 2013 *Berkshire   Hathaway   Letter   to Shareholders*

5. Gus Sauter, "Why aren't there more inves- tors like Warren Buffet?" http://www.sensible investing.tv/morelikewarrenbuffett

Chapter One

1. 1993 *Berkshire Hathaway Annual Report.*

2. 1996 *Berkshire Hathaway Annual Report.*

3. 2004 *Berkshire Hathaway Annual Report.*

4. Ibid.

5. James Altucher, *Trade Like Warren Buffett*, (New York: Wiley, 2005).

6. Mark   Sellers,   "Could   Stocks   Still   Be Undervalued?" February 18, 2004, http://

news.morningstar.com/articlenet/article.
aspx?id=104110

7. 2013 *Berkshire Hathaway Letter to Share-holders*

8. *Newsweek*, August 7, 1995.

9. William Sherden, *The Fortune Sellers* (New York: Wiley, 1998).

10. Ibid.

11. Ibid.

12. Philip E. Tetlock, *Expert Political Judgment* (Princeton, NJ: Princeton University Press, 2006).

13. Carl Richards, *The Behavior Gap* (New York: Penguin, 2012).

14. 1988 *Berkshire Hathaway Annual Report.*

15. 1991 *Berkshire Hathaway Annual Report.*

16. *BusinessWeek*, June 25, 1995.

17. 1996 *Berkshire Hathaway Annual Report.*

18. Dan Kadlec, "Warren Buffett Is Buying. Is It Time to Celebrate?" *Time*, November 09,

2011, http://moneyland.time.com/2011/11/09/warren-buffett-is-buying-is-it-time-to-celebrate/

19. 2008 *Berkshire Hathaway Chairman's Letter.*

20. 1990 *Berkshire Hathaway Chairman's Letter.*

Chapter Two

1. Adam Smith's "Money World" show, June 20, 1988, http://refspace.com/quotes/Warren_Buffett/investing

2. Clifford Asness, "Rubble Logic: What Did We Learn From the Great Stock Market Bubble", *Financial Analysts Journal* (November/December 2005).

3. http://www.buffettcup.com/Default.aspx?tabid=69

4. *BusinessWeek*, June 25, 1999.

Chapter Three

1. Brad Barber and Terrance Odean, "Boys Will Be Boys: Gender, Overconfidence and Common Stock Investment", *Quarterly Journal of Economics*, February 2001.

2. Ibid.

3. Brad Barber and Terrance Odean, "Do Investors Trade Too Much?" *American Economic Review* (December 1999).

4. Ibid.

5. Wilber G. Lewellen, Ronald C. Lease, and Gary G. Schlarbaum, "Patterns of Investor Strategy and Behavior Among Individual Investors," *Journal of Business*, 50, 1977, pp. 296–333.

6. Ibid.

7. Brad Barber and Terrance Odean, "Too Many Cooks Spoil the Profits", *Financial Analysts Journal*, January/February 2000.

8. *Smart Money*, June 2001.

9. Markus Glaser and Martin Weber, "Why Inexperienced Investors Do Not Learn: They Don't Know Their Past Portfolio Performance", July 2007.

10. Mark Carhart, "On Persistence in Mutual-fund Performance", *Journal of Finance* (March 1997).

11. Ibid.

12. Ibid.

13. Russel Kinnel, "How Expense Ratios and Star Ratings Predict Success", *Morningstar Adviser*, August 10, 2010.

14. Jonathan B. Berk, "Five Myths of Active Management".

15. 1993 *Berkshire Hathaway Annual Report.*

16. LGPS Structure Analysis, Hymans Robertson LLP, December 2013. https://www.gov.uk/government/uploads/system/uploads/attachment_data/file/307926/Hymans_Robertson_report.pdf

17. Amit Goyal and Sunil Wahal, "The Selection and Termination of Investment Management Firms by Plan Sponsors", May 2005.

18. Edwin J. Elton, Martin J. Gruber and Christopher R. Blake, "Participant Reaction and the Performance of Funds Offered by 401(k) Plans", *Journal of Financial Intermediation*, April 2007.

19. William Sharpe, "The Arithmetic of Active Management", *The Financial Analysts Journal*, January/February 1991, pp. 7–9.

Glossary

Active management The attempt to uncover securities the market has either under- or overvalued and/or the attempt to time investment decisions to be more heavily invested when the market is rising and less so when the market is falling.

Alpha A measure of risk-adjusted performance relative to a benchmark. Positive alpha represents outperformance. Negative alpha represents underperformance. Positive or negative alpha may be caused by luck, manager skill, costs and/or wrong choice of benchmark.

Annualised return The average return per annum on an investment over a given time period.

Arbitrage The process by which investors exploit the price difference between two exactly alike securities by simultaneously buying one at a lower price and selling the other at a higher price (thereby avoiding risk). This action locks in a risk-free profit for the arbitrageur — the one engaging in the arbitrage. The trading activity of arbitrageurs eventually eliminates these price differences.

Asset allocation The process of determining what percentage of assets should be dedicated to which specific asset classes. Also, the end result of this process.

Asset class A group of assets with similar risk and expected return characteristics. Cash, debt instruments, real estate and equities are examples of asset classes. Within a major asset class, such as equities, there are more specific classes, such as large and small company stocks and domestic and international stocks.

Basis point One one-hundredth of 1 per cent, or 0.0001.

Benchmark An appropriate standard against which mutual funds and other investment vehicles can be judged. Domestic large-cap growth funds should be judged against a large-cap growth index such as the FTSE 100 Index, while small-cap managers should be judged against a small-cap index such as the FTSE SmallCap Index.

Bid-offer spread The bid is the price at which you can sell a security, and the offer the price you must pay to buy a security. The spread is the difference between the two prices and represents the cost of a round-trip trade (purchase and sale) excluding commissions.

Book value An accounting concept reflecting the value of a company based on accounting principles. It is often expressed in per share terms. Book value per share is equal to book equity divided by the number of shares.

Book-value-to-market value (BtM) The ratio of the book value per share to the market price per share, or book value divided by market capitalisation.

Capital appreciation The increase or decrease in £ value of all securities in the portfolio for a specified period.

Cash invested £ amount of all purchases not including reinvested dividends/interest/capital gains.

Closet index fund An actively managed fund whose holdings so closely resemble the holdings of an index fund that investors are unknowingly paying larger fees for minimal differentiation.

Coefficient of correlation A statistical term describing how closely the price movements of different securities or asset classes are related. The higher the coefficient, the stronger the relationship between price movements of the two securities/ asset classes.

Commodity A physical good (such as corn, oil or gold) that is supplied without significant qualitative differentiation.

Compensated risk Risk that cannot be diversified away (like the risk of owning stocks). The market rewards investors for accepting compensated risk with a risk premium (a greater *expected* return) commensurate with the amount of risk accepted.

Convertible Security that can be exchanged for a specified amount of another, related security, at the option of the issuer or the holder (i.e. a **Convertible Bond** can be converted into a company's ordinary shares).

CPI Consumer price index. A measure of price inflation.

Currency risk The risk that an investment's value will be affected by changes in exchange rates.

Current yield The ratio of the coupon rate on a bond to the current price expressed as a percentage. Thus, if you pay par, or 100p on the £, for your bond and the coupon rate is 6 per cent, the current yield is 6 per cent. If you pay 97 for your 6 per cent discount bond the current yield is 6.186 per cent (6 divided by 97). If you pay 102 for a 6 per cent bond the current yield is 5.88 per cent (6 divided by 102).

Current value For most securities, Current Value = Quantity × Current Market Price.

Data mining A technique for attempting to build predictive real-world models by discerning patterns in masses of historical data.

Debenture An unsecured bond backed by the issuer's legally binding promise to pay.

Default Failure to pay principal or interest in a timely manner.

Denomination The face amount of a security.

Derivative A financial instrument whose characteristics and value depend on the characteristics and value of an underlying investment, typically a bond, commodity, currency or equity.

Discount The percentage by which the market value of a bond is less than par or face value.

Distressed shares Shares with high book-to-market values and/or low price-to-earnings ratios. Another name for **Value shares**.

Diversification Dividing investment funds among a variety of investments with different risk/return characteristics to minimise portfolio risk.

Duration The percentage change in the price of a bond that can be expected given a percentage change in the yield on that bond. A higher duration number indicates a greater sensitivity of that bond's price to changes in interest rates.

Efficient market A state in which trading systems fail to produce expected returns in excess of the market's overall rate of return, because everything currently knowable about a company is already incorporated into its stock price.

Efficient market hypothesis A hypothesis that markets are efficient. (See **Efficient market**.)

Emerging markets The capital markets of less-developed countries that are beginning to acquire characteristics of developed countries, such as higher per capita income. Countries typically included in this category would be Brazil, Russia, India, China, South Africa, Mexico, Turkey, Thailand and South Korea.

Ending value Value of the portfolio at the end of a specified period, such as the end of the quarter or the end of the year.

Event risk The risk that something unexpected will occur (war, political crisis, flood or hurricane) negatively impacting the value of a security.

Exchange traded funds (ETFs) For practical purposes these act like open-ended, no-load mutual funds. Like mutual funds, they can be created to represent virtually any index or asset class. They are not actually mutual funds. Instead, these new vehicles represent a cross between an exchange-listed stock and an open-ended, no-load mutual fund. Like stocks (but unlike mutual funds) they trade on a stock exchange throughout the day.

Expense ratio The operating expenses of a mutual fund expressed as a percentage of total assets. These expenses are subtracted from the investment performance of a fund to determine the net return to shareholders. They cover manager fees, administrative costs, and, in some cases, marketing costs.

Financial Conduct Authority (FCA) A UK regulatory body for the financial services industry responsible for the conduct and regulation of all retail and wholesale financial services firms operating in the UK and also the UK markets regulator and listings authority.

FTSE A company owned by London Stock Exchange Group and a provider of stock market indices and data services.

FTSE 100 An index that measures the performance of the 100 largest companies listed on the London Stock Exchange.

FTSE All-Share An index representing the performance of all the companies listed on the London Stock Exchange.

Fundamental security analysis The attempt to uncover mispriced securities by focusing on predicting future earnings.

Gilts Fixed income or index-linked bonds issued by the Debt Management Office and backed by the UK Government.

Growth shares Shares with low book-to-market values and/or high price-to-earnings ratios.

Green investing Choosing to invest in companies having positive environmental records. Green investing is a special category of **Socially responsible** investing.

Growth shares Companies that have relatively high price-to-earnings (**P/E**) ratios or relatively low book-to-market (**BtM**) ratios — the opposite of value shares — because the market anticipates rapid earnings growth, relative to the overall market. We are interested in a stock's earnings ratios because academic evidence indicates that investors can expect to be rewarded by investing in value companies' stocks. They are considered to be riskier investments (compared with growth companies' stocks), so investors demand a "risk premium" to invest in them.

Hedge fund A fund that generally has the ability to invest in a wide variety of asset classes. These funds often use leverage in an attempt to increase returns.

High-yield bond See **Junk bond.**

Hybrid security A security with both equity and fixed-income characteristics. Examples of hybrids are convertible bonds, preference shares and junk bonds.

IFA (Independent Financial Adviser) An IFA works for their client and is not an agent or representative of any bank, insurance company, investment house or any other financial institution. All IFAs are authorised and regulated by the FCA.

Income Dividends and/or interest income.

Index fund A passively managed fund that seeks to replicate the performance of a particular index such as the FTSE 100 or FTSE All-Share. The fund may replicate the index by buying and holding all the securities in that index in direct proportion to their weight (by market capitalisation) within that index. The fund could sample the index — a common strategy for small-cap and total market index funds — and/or use index futures and other derivative instruments.

Internal rate of return (IRR) also known as Money weighted rate of return (MWR) The internal rate of return provides a measure of the growth of the portfolio in absolute terms. Size and timing of contributions and withdrawals of cash and securities influence IRR, as well as the performance of those securities. The IRR is useful for determining if the portfolio is growing fast enough to meet future needs or goals. In the absence of capital flows the **Time Weighted Rate of Return (TWR)** and the IRR are identical.

Investment gain Capital appreciation plus income less fees and/or other expenses.

Initial public offering (IPO) The first offering of a company's shares to the public.

Investment grade A bond whose credit quality is at least adequate to maintain debt service. Moody's Investors Service investment grade ratings are BAA and higher. Standard & Poor's are BBB and higher. Below investment grade ratings suggest a primarily speculative credit quality.

IPS Investment policy statement. This statement provides the investor's financial goals and the strategies employed to achieve them. Specific information on matters such as asset allocation, risk tolerance and liquidity requirements should be included in the IPS. An IPS becomes more powerful if it is in writing, dated and signed.

Junk bond A bond rated below investment grade. Also referred to as a **High-yield bond**.

Kurtosis The degree to which exceptional values, much larger or smaller than the average, occur more frequently (high kurtosis) or less frequently (low kurtosis) than in a normal (bell shaped) distribution. High kurtosis results in exceptional values called "fat tails." Low kurtosis results in "thin tails."

Large-cap Large-cap shares are those of companies considered big relative to other companies, as measured by their **Market capitalisation**. Precisely what is considered a "large" company varies by source. For example, one investment professional may define it as having a market cap in excess of £1 billion, while another may use £5 billion.

Leverage The use of debt to increase the amount of assets that can be acquired (for example, to buy shares). Leverage increases the riskiness as well as the expected return of a portfolio.

Leveraged buy-out (LBO) An acquisition of a business using mostly debt and a small amount of equity. Assets of the business secure the debt.

Liquidity A measure of the ease of trading a security in the market.

Loser's game A game in which the odds of winning are so low it does not pay to play.

Management fees Total amount charged to an account for management of a portfolio.

Markdown The difference between a retail investor's selling price and the wholesale price (the price in the interdealer market).

Market cap/market capitalisation For an individual share this is the total number of shares of common stock outstanding, multiplied by the current price per share. For example, if a company has 100 million shares outstanding and its current stock price is £30 per share, the market cap of this company is £3 billion.

Maturity The date on which the issuer promises to repay the principal.

Mispricing. Active investors believe that markets misprice assets and they can take advantage of this. The **efficient market hypothesis** states that the market price of assets accurately reflects all publicly available information, and that mispricing to an extent that would enable you to get a better return than the market at the same level of risk does not occur.

Modern portfolio theory (MPT) A body of academic work founded on four concepts. *First*, markets are too efficient to allow expected returns in excess of the market's overall rate of return to be achieved consistently through trading systems. Active management is therefore counterproductive. *Second*, over sustained periods, asset classes can be expected to achieve returns commensurate with their level of risk. Riskier asset classes, such as small companies and value companies, will produce higher returns as compensation for their higher risk. *Third*, diversification across asset classes can increase returns and reduce risk. For any given level of risk, a portfolio can be constructed producing the highest expected return. *Fourth*, there is no one right portfolio for every investor. Each investor must choose an asset allocation that results in a portfolio with an acceptable level of risk for that investor's specific situation.

Money Weighted Rate of Return (MWR) See **Internal Rate of Return (IRR)**

Mortgage-backed security (MBS) A financial instrument representing an interest in a pool of mortgage loans.

Mutual fund is a collective investment vehicle in which the funds of numerous investors are pooled and managed in accordance with stated investment objectives, for example unit trusts, OEICs and SICAVs.

Net contributions Cash deposits plus the market value of securities deposited into the portfolio minus all cash withdrawals and the market value of securities transferred out.

Negative correlation When one asset experiences above average returns the other tends to experience below average returns, and vice versa.

Nominal returns Returns that have not been adjusted for inflation.

OEIC An Open Ended Investment Company is a UK mutual fund with variable share capital, i.e. shares can be issued and cancelled according to demand. OEICs are single priced with no bid–offer spread and they are regulated by the FCA.

P/E ratio The ratio of share price to earnings per share. Stocks with high P/E ratios are considered growth stocks; stocks with low P/E ratios are considered value stocks.

Par value The issue price of a share or bond. It is the same as **nominal value** and has no relation to the market price.

Passive asset class funds Mutual funds that buy and hold common stocks within a particular domestic or international asset class. The amount of each security purchased is typically in proportion to its capitalisation relative to the total capitalisation of all securities within the asset class. Each stock is held until it no longer fits the definition and guidelines established for remaining in that asset class. Passive asset class funds provide the building blocks needed to implement a passive management strategy.

Passive management Passive management is a buy-and-hold investment strategy, specifically contrary to active management. Characteristics of the passive management approach include lower portfolio turnover; lower operating expenses and transactions costs; greater tax efficiency; consistent exposure to risk factors over time; and a long-term perspective.

Preference shares have a fixed dividend but do not usually have any voting rights. If the company is wound up and there are sufficient assets, preference shares are usually repayable at par value, and take precedence over ordinary shares.

Premium The amount, if any, by which the price exceeds the principal amount (**par value**) of a bond.

Principal The face value of a bond, exclusive of interest.

Purchases In clients' reports from their advisers or broker/dealers, purchases represent the £ amount of a particular position purchased during a specified period.

Quantity In clients' reports from their advisers or broker/dealers, the quantity represents the number of a security's shares, units or option contracts held on the "as of" date.

Ratio of return to risk is a measure of a portfolio's efficiency calculated by dividing the annual return by the annual standard deviation.

Real returns Returns adjusted for inflation.

Rebalancing The process of restoring a portfolio towards its original asset allocation. Rebalancing can be accomplished either through adding newly investable funds or by selling portions of the best performing asset classes and using the proceeds to purchase additional amounts of the underperforming asset classes.

Real estate investment trust (REIT) As represented by REITs, real estate is a separate asset class. REITs have their own risk and reward characteristics, as well as relatively low correlation with other equity and fixed income asset classes.

Investors can purchase shares of a REIT in the same way they would purchase other equities, or they can invest in a REIT mutual fund that is either actively or passively managed.

Redemption The process of retiring existing bonds at or prior to maturity. It also refers to redeeming shares in a mutual fund by selling the shares back to the sponsor.

Reinvestment risk The risk future interest and principal payments when received will earn lower than current rates.

Risk premium The higher expected (not guaranteed) return for accepting a specific type of non-diversifiable risk.

Retail funds Mutual funds sold to the public, as opposed to institutional investors.

Sales/cash dividends In clients' reports from their advisers or broker/dealers, the £ amount of a particular position sold during a specified period. This figure will include any dividends paid in cash.

Serial correlation The correlation of a variable with itself over successive time intervals. Also known as autocorrelation.

Sharpe ratio Devised by William Sharpe, a measure of the return earned above the rate of return on riskless one-month US Treasury bills relative to the risk taken, with risk being measured by the standard deviation of returns. Example: The average return earned on an asset was 10 per cent. The average rate of one-month Treasury bills was 4 per cent. The standard deviation was 20 per cent. The Sharpe Ratio would be equal to 10 per cent minus 4 per cent (6 per cent) divided by 20 per cent, or 0.3.

Short selling Borrowing a security for the purpose of immediately selling it. This is done with the expectation the investor will be able to buy the security back at a later date (and lower price), returning it to the lender and keeping any profit.

SICAV (Société d'Investissement à Capital Variable) is a continental European mutual fund with variable share capital, i.e. shares can be issued and cancelled according to demand. SICAVs are usually single priced with no bid–offer spread.

Skewness A measure of the asymmetry of a distribution. Negative skewness occurs when the values to the left of (less than) the mean are fewer but *farther* from the mean than values to the right of the mean. For example: The return series of -30 per cent, 5 per cent, 10 per cent, and 15 per cent has a mean of 0 per cent. There is only one return less than zero per cent, and three higher; but the negative one is much further from zero than the positive ones. Positive skewness occurs when the values to the right of (more than) the mean are fewer but *farther* from the mean than are values to the left of the mean.

Small-cap Small-cap shares are those of companies considered small relative to other companies, as measured by their **Market capitalisation**. Precisely what is considered a "small" company varies by source. For example, one investment professional may define it as having a market cap of less than £500 million while another may use £1 billion. We are interested in a share's capitalisation because academic evidence indicates that investors can expect to be rewarded by investing in smaller companies' shares. They are considered to be riskier investments than larger companies' shares, so investors demand a "risk premium" to invest in them.

Spread The difference between the price a dealer is willing to pay for a bond (the bid) and the price a dealer is willing to sell a bond (the offer).

Socially responsible investing (SRI) Investment strategy seeking to maximise both financial return and social good.

S&P 500 Index A market-cap weighted index of 500 of the largest US stocks, designed to cover a broad and representative sampling of industries.

Standard deviation A measure of volatility or risk. The greater the standard deviation, the greater the volatility of a portfolio. Standard deviation can be measured for varying time periods, such as monthly, quarterly or annually.

Structured Investment Products are packaged products which may consist of one or more investment instruments such as derivatives, shares, options, indices and commodities. They are often complex and can be very high risk.

Style drift Style drift occurs when the portfolio moves away from its original asset allocation, either by the purchase of securities outside the particular asset class a fund represents or by not rebalancing to adjust for significant differences in performance of the various asset classes in the portfolio.

Systematic risk Risk that cannot be diversified away. The market must reward investors for taking systematic risk or they would not take it. That reward is in the form of a risk premium, a higher *expected* return than could be earned by investing in a less risky instrument.

Term to maturity The number of years left until the maturity date of a bond.

Three-factor model Differences in performance between diversified equity portfolios are best explained by the amount of exposure to the risk of the overall stock market, company size (market capitalisation), and price (book-to-market [**BtM**] ratio) characteristics. Research has shown that, on average, the three factors explain more than 96 per cent of the variation in performance of diversified US stock portfolios.

Time weighted rate of return (TWR) A rate-of-return measure of portfolio performance giving equal weight to each period regardless of any differences in amounts invested in each period. The TWR removes the impact caused by timing and the size of all capital flows. Because an investment manager typically has no control over contributions and withdrawals, the TWR is more suitable than the **Internal Rate of Return (IRR)** for determining the relative skill of the manager, or to compare to a market index or other managers. In the absence of capital flows, **TWR** and **IRR** are identical.

Tracking error The amount by which the performance of a fund differs from the appropriate index or benchmark. More generally, when referring to a whole portfolio, the amount by which the performance of the portfolio differs from a widely accepted benchmark, such as the FTSE 100 Index or FTSE all-share Index.

Transparency The extent to which pricing information for a security is readily available to the general public.

Treasury bills Treasury instruments with a maturity of up to one year. In the UK Treasury Bills are issued by the Debt Management Office which is an Executive Agency of Her Majesty's Treasury. They are issued at a discount to **par** and interest is paid in the form of the price rising toward **par** until maturity. They are backed by the UK Government.

Turnover The trading activity of a fund as it sells securities and replaces them with new ones.

Uncompensated risk Risk that can be diversified away, like the risk of owning a single stock or sector of the market. Since the risk can be diversified away, investors are not rewarded with a risk premium (higher expected return) for accepting this type of risk. Also called **unsystematic risk**.

Unit trust An open-ended UK mutual fund in which an investor holds units (not shares). The fund is established under a trust deed and units in the fund usually have a bid-offer spread. In the UK, unit trusts are regulated by the FCA.

Unsecured bond A bond backed solely by a good faith promise of the issuer.

Unsystematic risk See **Uncompensated risk**.

Value shares The shares of companies with relatively low price-to-earnings (**P/E**) ratios or relatively high book-to-market (**BtM**) ratios — the opposite of growth shares. The market anticipates slower earnings growth, relative to the overall market. They are considered to be riskier investments than growth companies' stocks, so investors demand a "risk premium" to invest in them.

Variable annuity A life insurance annuity contract providing future payments to the holder. The size of the future payments will depend on the performance of the portfolio's securities as well as investor's age at the time of "annuitisation" and prevailing interest rates.

Venture capital An investment in a start-up firm or small business, prior to its initial public offering. Typically entails a high degree of risk.

Volatility The standard deviation of the change in value of a financial instrument within a specific time horizon. It is often used to quantify the risk of the instrument over that time period. Volatility is typically expressed in annualised terms.

Weight Percentage value of a security or asset class held in a portfolio, relative to the value of the total portfolio.

Yield curve Graph depicting the relationship between yields and current term to maturity for fixed income investments with approximately the same default risk.

Zero-coupon bond A discount bond on which no current interest is paid. Instead, at maturity, the investor receives compounded interest at a specified rate. In taxable accounts, the difference between the discount price at purchase and the accreted value at maturity is not taxed as a capital gain, but is considered interest and usually taxed each year, not deferred until maturity.

Sources

The following are the sources for data contained in the text:

Morgan Stanley for data on the MSCI World ex-UK Index, www.msci.com. Used with permission.

FTSE for data on the FTSE All Share Index, FTSE NAREIT Equity REITs TR Index and FTSE British Government Index, www.ftse.com. Used with permission.

Dimensional Fund Advisers for data on the Dimensional UK Value Index, Dimensional UK Small-Cap Index, Dimensional International ex-UK Value Index and Dimensional International ex-UK Small Index. Dimensional index data simulated by Dimensional from Bloomberg securities and Fama/French data. This material has been distributed by Dimensional Fund Advisers Ltd., which is authorised and regulated by the Financial Conduct Authority. Past performance is no guarantee of future results. http://www. dimensional.com. Used with permission.

Acknowledgments

F or all their support and encouragement, I would like to thank the principals of BAM Advisor Services: Adam Birenbaum, Ernest Clark, Madaline Creehan, Thelia Eagan, Bob Gellman, Ed Goldberg, Joe Goldberg, Mont Levy, Vladimir Masek, Bert Schweizer III, Al Sears, Brent Thomas and Brenda Witt.

Thanks also go to those that read early drafts of this book and made significant contributions: Wendy Cook, Eric Ess, Jo-Ann Gallerstein, Mike Going, Kevin Grogan, Matt Hall, Stephen High, Scott Lucia, and Alex Madlener.

And a special thanks to Carl Richards for providing the inspiration for my drawing for Chapter 8, as well as the other illustrations.

I would also like to thank Igors Alferovs and Richard Wood, directors of Barnett Ravenscroft Wealth Management (BRWM) and Mary Whitehouse, the company's marketing consultant, who edited the UK edition of the book, adapting the original content based on the differences in taxation laws and financial planning techniques. Thank you also to Tim Hale from Albion Strategic Consulting, who helped crunch the numbers for the portfolios in Chapter 6. Their assistance was invaluable.

RC Balaban, my co-author of *Investment Mistakes Even Smart People Make*, helped with the initial drafts of the original US edition. If you enjoyed this book, RC deserves much of the credit.

I also thank my agent Sam Fleischman for all his efforts over the years and for getting me started as an author. I am forever grateful for his support and friendship.

I especially thank my wife Mona, the love of my life. Walking through life with her has truly been a gracious experience.

Index